# SILENT
# SISTERS

# SILENT SISTERS

*by Joanne Lee*
*with Ann and Joe Cusack*

MIRROR BOOKS

First published by Mirror Books in 2019

Mirror Books is part of Reach plc
10 Lower Thames Street
London EC3R 6EN
England

www.mirrorbooks.co.uk

© Joanne Lee

The rights of Joanne Lee to be identified as the author
of this book have been asserted, in accordance with the
Copyright, Designs and Patents Act 1988.

ISBN 978-1-912624-30-0

Ev
rep                                                                        e

This book is dedicated to the angels:
Baby John Lee
Angela Sheila
Katie Ann
Elizabeth Julia
Angelica Helen

# PROLOGUE

I switched off the engine, sucked in my breath and, for what would be my last moment of peace, I rested my head on the steering wheel. I had wrestled all night long with the decision. It was wrong and it was right; perhaps in equal measure. But all I knew, in absolute certainty, was that the body of my baby sister could no longer remain in a bin inside my mother's wardrobe. She deserved dignity and respect. She needed a proper burial. And there was nobody else to do it, except me. I clicked the car door shut and went up the path to mum's door. She stepped out into the sunshine without a word, a canvas bag looped casually over her arm, as though she was carrying shopping.

"Shall I take it?" I asked.

Mum didn't look at me but shook her head sharply. I was fixated, fascinated by the bag. It was a 'weekly shop' sort of bag. A bag for life. And now a bag for the end of life. It was to be an eco-friendly funeral then, I told myself with a mirthless chuckle. As long as we were saving the environment, that was a bonus.

"Would that count for me in court?" I wondered.

I doubted it somehow.

I opened the car boot, and, as I turned to take the bag, I noticed, in horror, that it was dripping. Thick globules of sticky red tell-tale mucus slurped onto the pavement, one by one. I looked around wildly, checking for passers-by, then took the bag as quickly as I felt was respectful. Mum didn't even seem to notice. I snapped the boot shut and looked at my jeans – my new beige jeans.

"Beige!" I shrieked silently. "You fool, Joanne."

The practicalities of burying a baby all by myself were mind-boggling and I hadn't thought it through well at all. I had sandals on too. Great planning. The cemetery was a short drive away, little more than 10 minutes. Mum sat in the passenger seat and didn't say a single word. But the stench from the car boot was making me gag. My eyes were streaming in protest. It was a thick mix of menstrual blood and rotting flesh; the start of life and the end of death. I could taste it, right down to my stomach. It was a revolting, repulsive smell. And it was my little sister, Helen. Retching as I drove, I screeched to a halt outside a corner shop and ran in to buy an air freshener.

"Sorry," I muttered, spraying myself and the whole car.

Mum looked at me in mild surprise. She didn't seem at all affected by the smell. Or indeed the occasion. Blinded by tears, and heaving uncontrollably, I found a parking place at the cemetery and stumbled outside, gulping in the fresh air. And then it hit me. And this was even worse than the smell. All around us, people were milling about tending graves and planting flowers. There was even a couple of little boys playing football on one of the paths. It was bright and sunny and people were making the most of the weather. The enormity – the horror – of what I was about to do engulfed me. And though I was out in the fresh air, away now from the stench, I felt more nauseous than ever before.

"Let me carry the bag," I said to mum. "It's busy here."

"No," she said flatly.

We couldn't start arguing, not here. I knew what she was like, all too well. Instead, I passed her the white bag, by now stained a dirty red-brown colour at the bottom, and I walked slowly behind her. The hairs on the back of my neck stood on end as we passed dog walkers and families. I fully expected someone to say: "What's that smell? What the hell have you got in that bag?"

I didn't for a minute think we could get away with this. But somehow, inch by inch, we moved forward unchallenged, so slowly we could have been on freeze frame in a horror film. I felt like I was walking through landmines.

"One false move," I breathed. "Just one and we've had it."

And then, suddenly, we were there. Our family grave. Nanna Winnie was buried here, along with my Uncle Bernard, and my own beloved baby son, John. I had been here just a couple of weeks earlier, with flowers for John on his birthday. I could never in my most disturbing of nightmares have dreamed that I would be back here – for this. First John. Now Helen. The grave was becoming some sort of mecca for dirty little secrets. A nerve centre of criminal depravity. I knelt down, fussing fraudulently with the flowers, picking out the odd weed. I felt like a sneak thief, waiting for the right moment to pounce.

"Hello, John," I said under my breath. "Forgive me, darling. Forgive me."

Mum stood, impassively, at the side of the grave. She was clutching the bag tightly to her stomach, her knuckles white, as though she was trying to hold on. It was impossible to tell whether she was reciting silent prayers or she was running through next week's shopping list in her head.

"She's no help," I told myself. "She never has been. She won't start now."

There was nothing for it. I had to start digging. I hadn't brought a spade, for obvious reasons. Digging at a grave, with a garden spade, might just ring alarm bells. I scrabbled at the earth with my bare hands, my fingers soon raw and bloody, but I didn't feel a thing. My beige jeans were muddy and damp and I cursed myself yet again.

"You'll know better next time," I told myself. "What? Next time!"

It was a hilarious, ridiculous, horrible thought. I scratched and scraped away at the earth, at first checking around me every few seconds, terrified of being rumbled by an on-looker. I had my response well-rehearsed in case

I was challenged: "Just digging a hole for some plants," I would say. "Lovely day for a spot of gardening."

But, as my heart beat faster and the sweat poured down my face, the people around me blurred and vanished. I forgot about mum. I focussed only on the earth beneath me. I thought of Nanna Winnie. Of my beloved John. Of vicious Uncle Bernard. And now, of poor little Helen, my dead sister, gone before she had even arrived.

"Pass me the bag," I said breathlessly.

I had dug about a foot and a half down, and I felt that would be enough. Any more and I was frightened of hitting Bernard's coffin. The thought sent shivers through me.

"Where's the head?" I asked quietly.

Mum pointed and handed me the canvas bag. My hand cupped around what was unmistakeably her skull, through the layers of the bag, I laid her down gently and whispered a prayer. The smell was hideous, even in the open air and I felt it stabbing at the back of my throat.

"Forgive me," I whispered again.

Then, like a maniac, I began covering her with mud and soil, throwing it through the air, desperately, haphazardly, so it splatted me in the eyes and mouth. I wanted it over. When I was finished, I stood up, weary and exhausted. Every inch of me ached. I wept.

"Do you want to say anything?" I asked mum, quietly. "A little prayer?"

She shook her head and turned to walk back to the car. It was as though she had been humouring me, playing along, for my sake. And now, enough was enough. Job done. She wanted to get home.

"You're going to jail, Joanne," said a voice in my head. "Too late now. You're going to jail."

I thought of my own two young daughters, waiting at home, and I was swamped with guilt and regret. If I had done the right thing, why did I feel so wretched? So scared? I felt infected. I had thought that burying the baby would bring a sense of dignity and peace. But I now felt as though I would never be clean again. And the smell. God, the smell. It hung from me, oozed from me, crawled all over me. All the way home, I sprayed the air freshener as I drove until it ran out, and then I kicked it onto the floor, underneath the pedals. I stank. Inside as well as out. And I knew no amount of washing, showering and scrubbing would ever get rid of it.

# CHAPTER 1

Ours was a small, cramped second-floor flat, dark and rather dingy. To a confused three-year-old it seemed as though day-light never came, and that scared me. But later I would realise that my mum, Bernadette, hardly ever opened the curtains. The furniture was cheap and second-hand and we had a black, plastic couch which stuck to the backs of my legs if I sat there too long and left me yelping in pain when I jumped up. I lived there with mum and my dad, Michael. Or so I was told, but I hardly ever saw him. I would convince myself, as a fanciful four-year-old, that perhaps he had some mystical qualities which meant he couldn't be seen at the flat. Maybe he was a wizard. His nickname, though, was 'The Milky Bar Kid', because of his striking blonde hair, blue eyes and round-rimmed glasses. He and mum had been teenagers when I was born, and I spent a lot of time with both sets of grandparents, whilst they were at work or at college, or perhaps just out on the town, trying to forget their responsibilities. Dad, when he magically appeared, was warm, kind and loving. Every time I saw him, he would pull me into his arms and lift me up for a cuddle. Yet he was strict too. But I didn't mind that. I knew exactly where I was with him. We had rules and boundaries; discipline and love, and that was comforting for a little girl. Once, when he caught me sneaking out into the road, he gave me the biggest telling off I'd ever had.

"You know you're not allowed to cross on your own," he shouted. "That's naughty."

It was him who instilled in me, at that young age, the difference between right and wrong and, even more importantly, having the courage to step up and say so. It was quite simple to me back then. Stay on the pavement and stay out of trouble. But as I got older, those lines would become blurred and fuzzy, right and wrong bleeding into one another, merging and overlapping. More often than not, I found myself doing the wrong things for the right reasons. And occasionally, the wrong things for the wrong reasons. And so what did that make me? But by then, dad was long gone and there was no moral compass, except my own, to keep me on track.

With dad's strict rules came a soft heart and one night, my border collie, Cindy, went missing. I was inconsolable, crying at the window, while mum flicked through her magazines on the sofa behind me. It was only when dad got home from work that he pulled on his coat and went out looking in the fields around our home.

"Don't worry, Joanne," he said, ruffling my hair. "I'll find her."

And sure enough, hours later, I heard Cindy's bark, and the sound of dad kicking his wellies off in the hallway.

"Safe and sound," he grinned.

I threw my arms around him and the smell of him, warm, safe, a faint whiff of aftershave, filled me with such contentment. Mum didn't look up from her magazine but then I didn't look at her either. I didn't include her and I didn't need her. Out of bravado, I pulled out a metaphorical tongue. I had my daddy, and that was enough. So perhaps he was a wizard, after all. The summer after my third birthday, we went away on holiday in a red Renault, all the way to Cornwall. It felt like we were going to the ends of the earth, but seeing mum and dad, chatting, giggling in the front seats was enough to keep me happy. Dad switched on the radio and mum sang along to the 70's hits – The Rolling Stones and Elton John.

I was curled up in a sleeping bag on the back seat, cosy and safe, and I didn't really care how long the journey took. Mum had long, brown hair and she kept flicking it back, over her shoulder and laughing at dad's jokes. I felt a fleeting sense of sadness that she had never paid me attention like that. But in the next instant, it was forgotten, as dad wound down his window and shouted, "Look, Joanne, we can see the sea! There's the seaside!"

I stuck my head out of the window, inhaling the salt and the excitement.

"Wow!" I shouted.

If it had been the Taj Mahal, or the Egyptian pyramids, my elation could not have been greater. We stayed in a small seaside hotel, making sandcastles on the beach, fishing in rock pools and paddling in the sea. One day, we went to visit a model village. Somehow, my hand slipped from dad's and I found myself wandering around, lost.

But even at three years old, I had a strong sense of independence and self-assurance.

"If they don't come back, I'll just live here, by the sea," I decided.

I sat on a small fence, watching the model steam train, confident that somehow I would manage and things would work themselves out. Sure enough, I spotted dad's blonde head amongst the tourists and soon he was carrying me along in his arms. My adventure was over, with a happy ending.

"You can't live here, Joanne," dad joked. "You won't fit in one of these tiny houses!"

We laughed together, but as I looked over dad's shoulder, I saw mum trailing behind, glassy-eyed and stony-faced.

Back at home, dad seemed to magically disappear once again. Late at night, tucked up in bed, I'd sometimes hear him come home from work and his voice was raised and angry. Him and mum were arguing a lot. I'd hear her screaming and wailing like a banshee, crockery smashing and doors slamming, and I would cover my ears with a pillow to shut out the noise. But I was anxious always to stay awake, to keep an eye on them. It was almost as if I, aged four, was the unofficial mediator. I worried that if I fell asleep, something bad might happen. The responsibility was all mine.

The months wore on and so did the rows, until I gradually grew used to them. I would tut in despair as I heard them bawling and swearing in the next room. I was a toddler, but well into middle-age in many respects.

We were soon on the move again and I wasn't sad to see the back of the dark flat. Next, I found myself living in a peculiar little house, where the bathroom, a horrid shade of olive green, was in my bedroom, the two areas separated only by an archway. I was woken every night by dad brushing his teeth or mum stumbling in for a wee. I might as well have been sleeping in the middle of the street.

"I can't sleep here," I complained. "It's too noisy!"

Mum didn't listen. She rarely did. She didn't say much either, at least not to me. There were only two people who listened to every word I had to say; and they were both profoundly deaf. My dad's parents, Edith and John, were wonderfully warm and caring. Dad could sign, and I had learned sign language too, as a toddler, to communicate with them. I was unaware of the actual learning process; signing was almost my first language and it seemed to come naturally to me. And it wasn't lost on me, even as a little girl, that I had more conversations with them than with anyone else. Visiting Nanny Edith, my short little arms would sometimes ache at the length of our conversations.

I told her everything. And she never once told me she was too busy, too tired, or frankly, too bored, to listen.

"Tell me everything, darling," she would sign. "I want to know it all."

She had an old typewriter and would use it to type out spellings and grammar to teach me. Thanks to Nanny Edith and her typewriter, I learned to write and spell my own name before I even started school.

In years to come, she would pass the typewriter on to me and I treasured it. I would sit in front of it, pressing the old keys, loving the hypnotic clicking sounds they made. If I closed my eyes I was back there, in the stillness of Nanny Edith's front room, with her typing: 'Where, were, wear' on the typewriter, along with a definition of each word.

She was as bright and resourceful as she was kind and loving.

On my fifth birthday, I was due to start school for the first time. I had stayed with Nanny Edith the night before which was in itself a birthday treat. The next morning, I woke to see a small white desk and chalk board in my bedroom. Childish enthusiasm getting the better of me, I tumbled out of bed with the sheets knotted around my legs and tripped over. But nothing could have stopped me smiling that day. I loved that desk. I sat myself down and swung my legs, kicking the underside. The wood made a good sound and I laughed and laughed. I wrote my name on the chalk board over and over and rubbed it out with the sleeve of my pyjamas.

"You have to go to school," Nanny signed, chuckling. "The desk will still be here when you get home."

Nanny dressed me in a blue pinafore and a pink polo neck. Then Mum appeared at the front door, dishevelled and disinterested, smelling of stale smoke. She flopped onto Nanny Edith's lovely clean couch, whilst Nanny fussed with my hair. Mum looked so out of place in that nice living room, like the one mouldy orange in a bowl of fresh fruit. I half expected a stain on the couch when she stood up. She came out into the street to wave me off, and I threw her a wave and shouted: "Ta-ra!"

Truth be told, I was so desperate to start school, I didn't care at all about leaving her behind. Even then, our bond was frayed like a piece of old elastic. Deep down, or perhaps not so deep down, I was sure she couldn't wait to see the back of me, either. Funny, or not so funny, I had reached five years of age, yet I couldn't remember once sitting on her knee. She had never, in my short life, told me a bedtime story. There was no bedtime kiss. No cuddle on the sofa. She never even held my hand. The year before, I had cut my knee while out playing, and I went running in to mum, tears glistening in my eyes. She took a cursory glance and said, "You're fine."

Her words stung more than my knee. But like most kids, I was a quick learner. And I didn't go to her for comfort again. I knew better. Soon after, I got mumps and mum scowled at the inconvenience of it all. I was packed off to Nanny Edith's, where I lay on the couch, a soft blanket up to my chin and a row of dolls to keep me company. Nanny Edith, herself like the most beautiful, delicate china doll, would put her arms around me, her big blue eyes shining with love, and sign:

"Nanny's here, darling. Don't worry."

When I was with her was the only time I didn't worry. I wished I belonged there. In the world of clean sheets, freshly baked cakes and cuddles. There was a beautiful calm, a serenity and a peace which went much further than a simple lack of noise. Nanny Edith's home sparkled with that rare combination of homeliness and cleanliness. Even her cooker shone. I used to think her cooker smiled like she did. Our cooker at home was thick with decades of grime and grease, cremated baked beans and charcoaled bacon rind. Mum never cleaned anything. She never *did* anything.

"Can't be arsed. Can't be arsed."

It was her answer to most questions. Her favourite phrase.

Nanny Edith and Grandad didn't have much money, and their furniture was dated and dilapidated, but all the lovelier in its shabbiness. There was a little bottom-sized dent in the old couch I lay on and it was such a comfort; like I was sitting in a big squishy hand. The mumps had given me a fever and some days I could swear that Nanny glided past me, like an angel, a blaze of light and goodness behind her. If St Helens had a paradise, then this was it. And so I was bitterly disappointed when, a few days later, I started to feel better and mum arrived to pick me up. The doorbell rang and an orange light in the hallway flashed, to let Nanny

Edith know she had a visitor. My heart sank when I spotted who it was, on the doorstep.

"Come on," mum said dully, avoiding eye contact and looking at a spot somewhere over my shoulder. "Time to come home."

It wasn't that mum was particularly mean or bad tempered. She didn't pick on me. She didn't shout. But she hardly even noticed me. And the indifference was hard to take. To a little girl, any show of emotion would have been better than none at all. And so any affection that first morning, as I skipped up the street towards my new school, would have been completely fake – on both sides. I had been pushed off to fend for myself very early on in life. And now that a new wave was here to take me, I couldn't wait to sail away. I walked confidently into the school yard, half child, half middle-aged woman. Born streetwise. That was me. Once inside the classroom, my new teacher, Mrs Hand, chose me to stand up first and introduce myself to the other children. To everyone's amazement, I spelled out 'My name is J-o-a-n-n-e L-e-e' using sign language. Mrs Hand smiled, puzzled and impressed. But to me, that was perfectly normal. Soon, I was teaching the whole class sign language, like it was some new craze. I was so happy to be instantly popular because everyone wanted to know how to sign. And that was all thanks to Nanny Edith and Grandad John. And if I could have loved them more for it, I would have.

# CHAPTER 2

In September 1977, for my sixth birthday, I had asked for a Cindy doll's horse. I loved the dolls, I played for hours with mine, dressing and undressing her, and the horse was my heart's desire. Every time someone asked me what I wanted, it tripped off my tongue.

On the morning of my birthday there were two parcels, one from mum, and one from dad. I ripped them open at the same time, childish enthusiasm getting the better of me, and I was left with two Cindy horses – one in each hand.

"Two!" I shrieked, unsure whether to be extra-pleased or slightly disappointed.

Dad wasn't there. But mum glared and snapped: "This is your own fault. Why didn't you ask your dad for something different? You've ruined your birthday now."

I didn't understand how I was to blame, but I said nothing. A big tear rolled down my face and splashed onto the discarded wrapping paper. I had hoped mum might agree to exchange one of the horses, but she refused.

"This is of your own making," she said. "I'm not helping you out."

I quickly realised that the horse from dad had a distinctive white strand in the tail, so it was easily recognised. And that was the one I played with, every day. The horse from mum lay under my bed, dusty and forgotten.

One day after school, soon after my birthday, mum picked me up and said: "We're going to see Nanny Pat, today."

Pat Hurst was her own mother. I dreaded going to see her, because she was usually annoyed about something, and if she wasn't, she was about to be. She was a towering giant of a woman, six feet tall, lean, well turned out and supreme in the knowledge that she was always right. She didn't carry weight, because she believed over-eating was a sign of weakness. She was fiercely neat and precise, her floral blouses buttoned right up to the neck, her slacks, as she liked to call them, ironed with a harsh middle-crease.

"Moderation!" she liked to say pompously. "Moderation is the key!"

Mum didn't hold my hand or talk, the whole way there. I was brimming with stuff I wanted to tell her about my six-year-old's day. But she wasn't interested and I knew that. We got to Nanny Pat's and I sat myself on the couch and tried to look as neat and tidy as I could. The back room was for family and people of no importance, and this was where I sat every time we visited. Though Nanny Pat was a meticulous housekeeper, I noticed there were dog hairs on the cushions and the rugs. It was a flaw. A smear in the polish. But I didn't dare point it out. I twirled one around in my finger and thumb and listened to the loud, angry whispers in the hallway between mum and Nanny Pat.

Eventually, Mum appeared and sat down awkwardly close to me. She cleared her throat and managed a watery sort of smile.

"Come into the lounge," she said.

I stared – stunned. Nanny Pat's lounge, her 'parlour' was reserved for important people and The Priest. I'd had a glimpse in there several times, but I had never actually been inside. Nanny Pat had a small latch at the top of the door to prevent children with grubby hands gaining access. But today, I watched open-mouthed as she ceremoniously undid the latch and the door swung open quietly. There was a hush as we walked inside.

The walls were decorated with thick, green, embossed wallpaper and there was a fireplace with a marble hearth. With one eye on Nanny Pat, I flicked out a hand to stroke the wallpaper. It was irresistibly soft and fluffy and I'd never seen anything like it.

"Like pillows on the wall," I said to myself curiously.

But there was an overpowering smell of pot-pourri too and as I breathed in I felt like I was eating soap. The couch had been upholstered by hand, the cushions were embroidered. And there was not a speck of dust or dirt to be seen.

Nanny Pat nodded at the couch and I hesitated before perching on the end. Mum stood in front of me and said, all matter of fact, "Your daddy and I are getting divorced soon. You and me will live here, with Nanny Pat. Daddy will live somewhere else."

I nodded, distracted, and looked around me at the porcelain figures on the mantlepiece and the shining brass mirror hanging on the chimney breast.

"So," I thought. "This is what the lounge looks like! Wow!"

I was still bowled over by the smell of polish and air freshener when Nanny Pat ordered me back out and into the room with the dog hairs again. She clicked the lock back onto the lounge door and that was that. The full scale of mum's announcement didn't hit me at all. I didn't even know what a divorce was. It was probably no surprise to people around us. She and dad had married far too young and only after mum discovered she was pregnant with me. They had so many rows that to me, it was normal. In fact, them not having a row seemed rather peculiar. And of course, the two of them separately buying me the same birthday present should have been a warning light. But at that age, I felt quite pleased with the news, because it meant that we were moving house. Nanny Pat still had four of her teenage children living at home, and hers was a busy household. I hated being an only child, life at our house was lonely and far too quiet. Now, at last, I'd have the family I longed for.

Later that afternoon, dad came to Nanny Pat's house to see me. He and mum sat either side of me as though we were in church.

"Some people don't get along with each other," dad said. "Me and your mum have been arguing and we've decided it's better to split up."

I nodded, again, thinking about the embossed wallpaper in the lounge and how soft it had felt.

"I've got a job in London," he told me. "I'm going away, Joanne. I won't see you for a long time. I'll miss you so much."

He held me tight and I was surprised to see his cheeks were wet with tears and his glasses were steamed up. It was only then that I realised the enormity of what he was telling me.

"What about swimming?" I asked him, thinking of my first priority.

He and I went swimming twice a week. Dad had always been adamant that I should learn to swim and I was confident paddling alongside him in the big pool, before I had even started school. It wasn't mum's 'thing' she had always said. She and her brother, Bernard, had once got blind drunk in the local park and he had pushed her out across the lake in a rowing boat. She had screamed hysterically until help came, and she had been left with a morbid fear of water. So I knew there was no way she would take me swimming. In fact, there was no way she would take me anywhere at all.

"I'll write to you," dad promised, unable to meet my eyes.

"What about my Nanny Edith?" I asked, panic suddenly rising in my chest. "Will I still see her?"

Dad nodded and looked to mum. And in a rare show of compassion, she smiled and said: "You can see Nanny Edith every weekend, don't worry about that."

I was so grateful to her, for allowing me to go. As I got older, I would look back and guess that she was probably just relieved to off-load me and get me out of the way at weekends. It was an arrangement that suited her as much as me. Convenience, rather than compassion.

It was decided too that Cindy, my dog, would go and live with Nanny Edith. Mum couldn't cope with her and Nanny Pat had her own dogs. It was a wrench. I would miss Cindy. But at the same time, I was glad she would be close by.

We moved in with Nanny Pat later that same week.

"It's all for the best," mum said, as we packed bags and boxes and waited for Nanny Pat to come and collect us. It wasn't best for me. But I said nothing.

"You will have to share a bedroom," Nanny Pat rapped. "And I expect good behaviour. Or there will be trouble. I'll have your guts for garters, young lady."

She didn't raise her voice. She didn't need to. The image was a terrifying one, and though I wasn't sure what garters were, it sounded like a painful process.

Hers was a large, four bedroomed house, on a respectable, leafy road, at the edge of a park, the same park where mum had been stranded on the boating lake. Walking upstairs, carrying my own little bag with my Cindy dolls and horse inside, I suddenly stopped, frozen. The first bedroom, a box room, belonged to my Uncle Bernard. He was away in the army, but just the mention of his name was enough to strike fear into me. The bedroom door was shut, but there was a fusty, sweaty, smell, seeping from under the door.

My memories of him were of a drunken, loud, aggressive man. When he was home from the army, the whole atmosphere in Nanny Pat's house changed dramatically.

He was, without doubt, the blue-eyed boy of the family. Even as a little child I could see that he was her favourite, he had no chores to do and she never lost her temper with him.

At weekends, when we visited, he would be lying in bed, late in the morning, and we would have to tip-toe past his door, to the bathroom, terrified of waking him. He was like a sleeping cyclops.

When he did wake up, he was nothing but a bad-tempered bully.

"Where's my breakfast? Where's my brew?" he demanded.

He was vile with his siblings and rude to his parents. I didn't understand why Nanny Pat let him behave like that. It was as if he had a hold over her, as if she was wary of challenging him. But I had no idea why.

I was certain only of the fact that Bernard was an ogre and I didn't like him at all. I was glad that at least he wasn't here at the moment and wasn't expected home for a while.

Nanny Pat's voice floated up the stairs and I heard her telling mum, "You can have Bernard's room."

I felt a shiver. Mum followed me upstairs and as she opened the door, there was a sinister creak, and I caught sight of an old-fashioned orange bedspread. For some reason, orange seemed like a bad omen and I shivered again.

I shared a bedroom with my two aunts, Carmel, or Cab, as we called her, and Patricia, whose nickname was Dish. I loved the colour and the light in there. They were young women and the dressing table was littered with make-up and perfume and teen magazines. There were David Essex posters on the wall and a radio cassette player in the corner. We would gather round for the Top 40 countdown each week, singing along and dancing. For the songs they wanted to record, we had to stay deathly silent, hardly daring to even breathe, in case it was picked up on the recording.

I thought I was so *cool*. I couldn't believe my luck.

My aunts had high-heeled platform shoes in the wardrobe and at night, when I was supposed to be in bed, I would slip out of the crisp, starched sheets and try a pair on. It was difficult to be quiet, clomping around in someone else's shoes, many sizes too big, but it was worth the risk. I would look in the mirror, hold my hair up, and pull what I thought was a pout like my Cindy doll.

Our room was in-between Nanny Pat's and Granddad Bernard's room, and further along, my Uncle Peter's room. Me and my aunts would sit on the beds, trying on lipstick, and I would listen in awe to their stories about boyfriends.

But I knew, the moment I heard Nanny Pat on the stairs, that silence was absolutely necessary. She seemed to have bat-like hearing and if I so much as sneezed into my sheets she would bark through the adjoining wall, "Sleep now child or I will have your guts for garters!"

One of my aunts would usually walk me to school in the morning. Another would pick me up. This was a whole new routine for me, and I made the most of it. I was glad to leave mum at home each morning. I didn't need her at all. I didn't even see much of her at Nanny Pat's, there were plenty of aunts around instead to keep a surrogate eye on me.

"They're my big sisters," I told my school-friends proudly. "Aren't I lucky?"

But I soon learned that living with older siblings, make-believe or not, could be alarming, too. Sometimes in the evenings, when I was settling down to sleep, I'd listen to my aunts and uncle Peter sitting on the next bed, scaring each other with stories of the 'Middlehurst Curse.'

Middlehurst, I gleaned, was Nanny Pat's maiden name. And all the family believed she carried some kind of curse. Nanny Pat of course, knew nothing about it. Or at least she appeared to know nothing about it. And perhaps that was all part of the magic.

"There's a house further down our street, where people go in, but never come out," my Uncle Peter told me solemnly.

"It's the curse."

One afternoon, Peter came skipping through the front door, his face lit up with excitement.

"Passed my test!" he shouted. "I can officially drive!"

In celebration, he grabbed Nanny Pat's car keys for her green Mini and ran off outside to show off his new skills. Cab, Dish and I stood at the door, laughing. It was a celebration, but there was no denying a hint of terror in the air, too. Peter was taking a risk, driving her car. She had popped out on an errand but was expected back soon. Peter did a lap of the block, beeping the horn and waving out of the window like royalty, and we cheered back in reply. But as he returned for the final stretch, we were horrified to suddenly see Nanny Pat at the top of the street, her eyes swivelling as she spotted her own car driving up the street towards her. She stood, frozen still, as though the shock of being disobeyed and disrespected had paralysed her completely.

"He passed his test," I called, by way of explanation.

But as Nanny Pat drew closer, I could see she was not in the mood to celebrate with us. Peter slowed in the road outside, and swung expertly back into the driveway. But somehow he had misjudged the angle and instead smashed into the gate post.

There was a sound of rubble crunching, glass splintering, and then a horrible silence. I hardly dared look, as Nanny Pat, practically foaming at the mouth, began bawling and screeching at poor Peter. It was very unlike her to let her guard drop in public, she normally reserved all outbursts for the sanctity of the home, and so we knew this must be bad. She had gone totally and utterly ga-ga.

"She looks as though she's possessed," Cab whispered.

That was exactly it. Possessed. I was convinced she was bewitched by the Middlehurst curse.

Soon after, my aunt's boyfriend finished with her, and she screamed dramatically, "I invoke the Middlehurst curse upon him."

My mind went back to the dark, gloomy flat I had shared with my mum and dad and I wondered if that, too, was cursed. Was my mum cooking up spells in the darkness? The curtains were always closed and my dad was always out. Now, I could see, there was a sinister element to life there, that I had never spotted before. And were curses passed down, through generations? And if so, could I be next? I wasn't sure whether a curse was something you could politely refuse and pass on, or whether there was no choice in the matter. Would I inherit the Middlehurst curse, whether I wanted it or not?

They were mindboggling questions for an impressionable child. Long after the lights had gone out, and when my aunts were asleep, I would lie awake, rigid with fear, picturing my mother dropping live toads and wriggling cockroaches into a pan of boiling water.

Nanny Pat was such a fearsome figure and I could well imagine, at that age, her having some grisly link to the supernatural. I spent hour after terrified hour, in the dead of night, fretting about the family curse. The next morning,

Nanny Pat would bark me into consciousness and frighten me down the stairs for breakfast.

Though I knew better than to say it, I was just grateful not to be turned into a frog over my cornflakes.

Every Sunday and Holy Day, Nanny Pat attended church, and everyone under her roof was expected to do the same. She would drape a black, lace veil over her head and she had her own leather-bound prayer book. To me, she looked like a witch with a book of spells.

"It's the curse," I said to myself. "It has to be."

She dragged the whole family – mum excepted – along to church every Sunday morning at 10am. Mum didn't go to church and Nanny Pat never bothered her about it. Mum was rarely even out of bed in time for the Sunday service. Maybe, I decided, Nanny Pat thought mum was beyond redemption.

Nanny Pat would sweep into church, crossing herself sanctimoniously with a dash of holy water and kneeling briefly at the pew, before sitting down with a face like thunder. The statue of the Virgin Mary herself seemed to flinch as she walked past.

Mum and Dad had never been particularly religious and so this was all new to me. I had no idea what to do or even why I was there.

"Why's the priest wearing a dress?" I whispered loudly. "And why is he stood on a box?"

Nanny Pat gave me a murderous look.

"Be quiet," she hissed. "No fidgeting, child. No talking. You're in God's house now."

I would do my best to keep up with the congregation, standing, sitting and kneeling on demand. I was made to sing loudly too, and if I ever paused for a rest, Nanny Pat would hit me sharply on the back of the head. It worked a treat to set me off singing again, like kicking an old car to get it started. The priest himself spoke so slowly, so wearily, that I had to suppress the urge to run onto the altar and kick him too, to hurry him along. The mass took well over an hour because he dragged out every syllable like it was going to be his last. There were occasions when I actually wondered if he had died, mid-sermon, because his speech was so infuriatingly slow.

One week, as we knelt in prayer, I spotted a shiny 10 pence piece on the floor of the pew in front. It was tantalisingly close. I was sure if I wriggled under my bench, I could reach it. I thought of the 10 penny chews I could buy. Or the can of Dr Pepper. Or the quarter of strawberry bon bons. I had to have it. The problem was, Nanny Pat was watching me, her eyes boring right through me. Even when her eyes were closed, I was sure she could see me.

"I've eyes in the back of my head," she used to tell me.

And I believed her, too.

I waited until she was deep in prayer, and then I spotted my opportunity. I leaned forward, my fingertips just inches from the coin. I had just hooked my prize when, suddenly, I felt bony fingers yanking me backwards and I found my own face just inches from Nanny Pat's livid stare.

"It's not your money!" she seethed quietly.

A few moments later, the collection plate was passed down our pew and Nanny Pat nodded towards my hand and glared at me. It pained me dreadfully to drop my 10 pence into the church collection. But I had no choice. I was sure the priest would spend it on Horlicks or whatever old men drank and it was such a waste.

Every Sunday was ruined by our trip to church. But there was no way out of it. Easter came and we had to go almost every day. There was no let up – and there was more in store.

"It will soon be time for your First Communion," she told me seriously. "The most important day of your life."

Every Saturday, we would go out shopping, and though it wasn't as bad as church, there were moments of pure terror. One week, I asked for a new toy, as we made our way round the shops.

"Please," I wheedled. "Please, I want a toy."

Nanny Pat turned and swiftly walloped the back of my legs with a stinging slap. Then she thrust her face inches from mine and screamed, "I am not your Nanny Edith!"

I cried more from shock than from the pain of the punishment.

Life under Nanny Pat's thumb was stifling as well as scary. She was not a woman to be messed with. She worked as a nursing officer and she ran her ward and her home with the same military precision and tyrannical temper. The sound of her wooden Scholls, clacking down her posh parquet hallway, was enough to strike an unholy fear into all of us. She had a weak heart apparently. But it didn't show one bit. She would growl like a bull dog and sometimes I was terrified she would actually bite me too. Her home was clinical with cleanliness and orderly to the point of suffocation. The air itself was stiff with tension.

"Everything has its place!" she growled. "A clean house is a clean mind!"

If I so much as moved a cushion she would tut loudly. I felt like I was messing the place up just by being there. And what was more important than being clean, was being seen to be clean. What really mattered, to Nanny Pat, was how things looked. Pull back the curtain, and the façade crumbled. I was living in the Land of Oz.

"Rats Tails!" she spat, when she saw my hair, tangled in the same ponytail for days on end.

I had never been inside a hairdresser's in my life. I couldn't recall mum ever even washing my hair. It was all left to me. But Nanny Pat didn't scratch beneath the surface. She didn't confront mum about my hair or ask me why it was always such a mess. She tutted, marched me into the living room, and pulled a brush firmly through the knots. To my horror, she then did the same to my hair as I'd seen her doing with her own — spitting on her hands to dampen the ends of my hair before curling them around the brush.

It turned my stomach, knowing my head was dripping with her spit. But I couldn't object. It was more than my life was worth.

"There," she said, smug with self-congratulation. "Much better. Now don't let me see it looking a mess again."

Nurse Pat looked at the symptoms, not the cause. That way, she didn't have to look at herself too deeply, either. Her own hair was permanently in rollers. I would watch, in silent disgust, as she spat on the ends of her fingers then used them to stick a section of her hair to the roller. By the time she had finished, behind a cloud of hair spray, it was as rigid as the regime in her house. I used to imagine I could snap off her curls, one by one.

We each had a list of chores to do, in the house, and I was soon added to the rota. I had to clean the shoes, every Sunday evening. I had to water the flowers outside, using three drops of plant food, which I rather enjoyed. But I was also made to clean up all the dog poo from Nanny Pat's garden, which I found both disgusting and difficult. I was too little to carry the heavy shovel used for clearing away dog mess and often I would end up smearing it all over my hands and clothes before landing it into the bin.

"Child!" Nanny Pat would scream. "I will have your guts for garters if you come in my house covered in that muck!"

I had no choice but to rinse my hands off in freezing cold water in a bucket, outside the back door. My fingers were red raw and glowing with cold by the time I had finished.

But I was not the sort of child to let life, or Nanny Pat, get the better of me, and the next time I fed the plants, I poured almost half the bottle of plant food into my watering can, hoping the overdose would kill the lot.

"Serves you right, you old cow," I muttered, as I splashed it willy-nilly around the garden. When I told my aunts in bed, later that night, we giggled until our ribs hurt.

Nanny Pat was a fantastic cook, she believed in good, wholesome, traditional food and I was well fed there, with a thick helping of Catholic guilt slapped onto each meal.

"There are kids with nothing!" she would shout, demonic as she waved her serving spoon. "I want to see a clean plate or I will have your guts for garters!"

I wouldn't have dared leave a morsel. I had seen her hold my aunts' noses and force feed them carrots. I said nothing. I had also seen her adding a generous measure of Bacardi into her black coffee at the dinner table, but again, I kept quiet. Like I said, I was a quick learner. I had the measure of my mum. And now I had the measure of Nanny Pat. And I was smart enough to keep my head down and my opinions to myself.

"Children should be seen and not heard," Nanny Pat would remind me.

And my reply, honed to perfection, was of course, total silence.

At Nanny Pat's, I was well cared for. Well 'turned out' as she liked to say. But there were no kisses and cuddles. Nobody played with me, though my aunts certainly entertained me. But I certainly wasn't allowed to go out and get muddy or wet in the rain. If Nanny Pat beckoned me over, it was to spit on her hanky and wipe a smear off my cheek.

"Cleanliness costs nothing!" she rapped.

If my uniform wasn't to her liking, she would make me strip off at the door and iron it all over again. Never mind that I went to school with tears rolling down my cheeks and my little heart aching for a friendly word. As long as my shoes were polished and my hair was brushed, nothing else mattered. It was life's little trimmings that counted with Nanny Pat — hygiene, good grammar and impeccable manners. One day, I was running through her hallway and her big Alsatian dog, Ben, jumped up and bit my ear. I yelled in pain, blood dripping onto my shoulder and down onto my hands. I heard the sound of Nanny Pat's heels clacking on the wooden floor behind me and she grabbed me, pushed on the half-moon glasses which hung on a chain around her neck, and peered hard at the wound.

"We can't take her to hospital," she said. "Word will get out and the dog will be put down. I'll have to sew it myself."

Nobody argued with her. Nobody dared. My grandfather, Bernard, just buried his head deeper inside his newspaper. My heart was thudding out of my chest as Nanny Pat and her friend, Laura, held me down, by the living room window for best light. Nanny Pat's face was close to mine, and she smelled of hairspray and bleach. Grunting irritably, she punctured my ear with a needle. I clamped my mouth shut and bit down on a cushion. I knew without being told, I was not allowed to cry. But Nanny Pat felt my shoulders shaking and said, "Don't be a silly girl, it's just a little stitch."

Afterwards, she took off one of her wooden Scholls and battered the dog. It yelped and whined horribly, but Nanny Pat was a woman with focus and she did not stop until she was done. Granddad Bernard seemed to wrap the newspaper around his head, shrinking back into his chair as though he could disappear into the back of it.

Just the weekend before, Nanny Pat had made him put on a crash helmet and hang out of the bedroom windows, backwards, to paint the outside window frame. She had held his ankles, purple in the face and shouting out orders, which he couldn't hear because the helmet was covering his ears.

"I could have been killed," he said later.

Nanny Pat had shrugged, seemingly unconcerned. Her window frames were important. Everyone outside could see them.

Today, Granddad Bernard was out of the limelight, and he liked it that way. He was not a man given to shows of great courage or emotion and he was not about to come to my aid. Like the rest of us, he knew his place.

Nanny Pat showed him my bandages and said: "It had to be done."

He nodded meekly, showing approval, puffed on his pipe, and disappeared back behind his newspaper.

Two weeks after the bite, I had to make my First Holy Communion, still with bandages wound around my head.

"What happened to you?" my teacher asked with a frown.

Nanny Pat didn't like 'loose talk.' And so, I said nothing. It went no further. My religious teacher was probably just as scared of Nanny Pat as I was, anyway. And so he knew enough to leave well alone.

"Let's pray to the Lord to heal your poor head quickly," he said kindly.

As a nursing officer too, she had status and clout in the neighbourhood and not many would have challenged her. The only person Nanny Pat bowed down to, in the entire world, was The Local Priest. Even Ben the Alsatian seemed to cower, on cue, when the priest came round. He made a weekly visit and he was ushered into the lounge as the honoured guest, to sit side by side with the embossed wallpaper and the overpowering pot-pourri. Nanny Pat couldn't have made more fuss if it was St Peter himself popping in. Whilst he was there, I was warned not to make any noise. If I so much as breathed loudly, I was in for it.

"Not a peep out of you!" Nanny Pat warned as she waggled a finger, mottled like a chipolata sausage.

I was left standing in the hallway, listening to her fawning over the priest. I noticed, with interest, that he could speak at a normal pace when he wasn't saying mass and I wondered if he slowed down deliberately, just to make us all suffer.

"Father, could I bring you a brandy? Warms the soul on a cold day," I heard her saying.

She could switch in a flash from evil bully to simpering sycophant, the moment he knocked on the door. I marvelled at the change in her. As a child I was impressed by her acting skills, but I couldn't understand the reason behind it all.

It would only be years later when the hypocrisy hit me.

It felt as though I was only just getting settled in at Nanny Pat's when mum announced, just before I turned eight, that we were on the move yet again. And this time, we were off to our own home, just me and her, again in St Helens and not far away. It was a newly-built, three bedroomed terraced house, and from the outside it looked clean and welcoming. But inside, despite the newness, it was somehow dark and dreary, just like our old flat, and I didn't like it.

"It's the Middlehurst curse," I said to myself. "It's following us around."

I was sad to leave Nanny Pat's house behind. Because although I was frightened of her, I had enjoyed living there. Sharing a bedroom with my aunts had been wonderful. I appreciated having cooked dinners and clean clothes. And I liked a busy house, overflowing with people, with so many adults parenting me that I barely missed my own parents, who were both absent in different ways.

The new house was eerily quiet, and I immediately missed the hustle and bustle of Nanny Pat's. Besides, though Nanny Pat was fierce, she was also fiercely consistent. With her, I knew what to expect, and when to expect it. And that was a comfort for a child.

There was no routine at our new house. At first, mum seemed excited by the move, and she was full of energy.

She unpacked our clothes and helped me arrange my new bedroom.

"My own bedroom!" I beamed.

I knew I'd miss my aunts. But having my own room would be fun, too.

Those first few weeks, mum would shop for food most days. She kept the house tidy and she did my washing, though she never ironed.

There was still that same distance between us. An awkwardness. More than anything, I missed the closeness, the affection, from my aunts at Nanny Pat's house. They had plaited my hair, painted me with lipstick, tickled me till I screamed for mercy.

There was nothing like that with mum. There was no fun.

Without Nanny Pat to keep her in line, mum slipped, gradually, into a state of slovenliness. She stopped cleaning and washing. She rarely cooked.

"Can't be arsed," she would say, flopping onto the couch and lighting a fag.

With no other adults around, she could do – or rather not do – just as she liked. She drank most nights and lay in bed late each morning. After oversleeping once, and getting into trouble with my teacher, I quickly worked out I would need to fend for myself. I had to get myself up for school, do my own ponytail, wash my face and sort myself out.

Sometimes, I heard mum snoring and muttering in her sleep, as I brushed my teeth in the bathroom next to her room. And I felt a growing tide of resentment towards her.

Why couldn't she walk me to school, like other mums? Or at least stand at the front door, in her nightie, and wave me off down the street?

When I left the house, I'd shout a cheery: "Bye then!"

But it was more that I wanted to mark my departure to the rest of the world. I didn't want to be seen as poor little Joanne who sneaked out of the house, uncared for and unnoticed. I shouted out also because I wanted to try out my voice for the first time that day. I had nobody else to talk to, except myself.

I never expected mum to reply, and she never did.

Those mornings, I never ate breakfast, not once. By the age of eight, I could work the washing machine and iron my own uniform. I had picked up tips from my aunts, who did all the ironing at Nanny Pat's. I worked the washing machine out without too much trouble, too. Sure, I had my fair share of disasters. In one wash, I turned all my white school socks a tired and grimy grey. It would have been an unforgivable aberration in Nanny Pat's world. But mum didn't even notice, or if she did, she never referred to it.

I was happy to make my own mistakes, and look after myself, for the most part.

In the evenings, if mum was watching telly, I would stand on a chair, next to the stove, and empty a can of tomato soup into a pan. I could make toast too. As time went on, I got more adventurous and I would cook sausages and mash.

Mum would sometimes peer over my shoulder and offer some culinary advice. But she was too lazy to join in and help.

34

Even so, when it came to serving the meal, I always served up enough for two. I knew I should leave her out. It would serve her right. But I just couldn't bring myself to do it.

The washing up piled up in the sink and the dust gathered on the furniture. It was only when Nanny Pat was due to visit that mum would suddenly whip into a frenzy, throwing empty cans in the bin and tearing around with the hoover.

But Nanny Pat was not easily fooled. Despite her own secret tipples, she disapproved strongly of drinking. And in particular, drinking to excess. She spotted mum's failings easily, probably because she shared them herself.

"I hope you're not letting yourself down, Bernadette," she remarked darkly when she called in one day.

Mum was a dithering wreck in front of Nanny Pat and she shook her head firmly.

"We're doing fine, aren't we?" she said to me, slipping her arm around my shoulders. It was all for show, and I froze.

I wanted to shout: "She never puts her arm around me! She never speaks to me!"

But I just swallowed and stared wide-eyed at Nanny Pat.

Once when she called in, mum was wearing a tight T-shirt, probably shrunk in the washing machine in one of my disasters.

"Cover yourself, Bernadette!" Nanny Pat hissed. "Have some self-respect!"

She gave mum a good talking to while I hid upstairs, glad that mum was getting her come-uppance but worried that I might be next. In my naivety, I actually hoped that a telling-off might be the wake-up call that mum needed.

But after she had gone home, mum poured herself a large vodka and I realised, with a dull acceptance, that this was how it was going to be.

Mum drank too much, while I did too much: washing, ironing, cooking, cleaning.

It was me, too, who filled out all the letters from school and returned them. No school trips, no chess clubs. I couldn't be in the netball team or join the athletics club. I was needed at home to do the housework. One of my friends at school said to me one day: "My mum says your mum has made you old before your time."

Neither of us knew what it meant so we just laughed and carried on playing with her dolls. Another time, I was at her house when her mum brought in a pile of freshly ironed clothes and put them in a drawer. It was nothing more than that. But my mouth fell open in wonder.

"Does your mum do that for you all the time?" I asked enviously.

She nodded and I almost drooled with jealousy. I would have loved a collection of dolls, like my friend. But more than anything, I would have loved a mum like hers.

# CHAPTER 3

One night, it was just the two of us at home, when mum opened one of her puzzle books and said: "Do you fancy playing a game with me, Joanne?"

I would like to be able to say that I told her to sod off. That I reminded her she hadn't so much as held my hand for seven years. But, of course, I was a little girl, desperate for any scraps of affection that came my way, and especially so from my mother. And so I nodded eagerly, delightedly, and climbed up on the couch beside her. We did crosswords and wordsearches. And we played daft memory games. I loved it. There was no affection and hardly any conversation. But that didn't bother me. I treasured each moment of those evenings playing games, just me and her. I started to wonder if she was melting a little.

"Perhaps she likes me after all," I thought.

I had a habit, when mum was downstairs, of rooting through all her bedroom drawers. Maybe it had come from me growing up too soon and having a sense of responsibility for her. Or maybe I was just plain nosy. But one night, whilst she was watching TV, I came across a shaving brush in the top of the drawer. I knew, instantly, that it wasn't hers and I confided in my friends at school the next day.

"She's got a bloke," they said. "Only men have shaving brushes."

I shook my head firmly.

"No way," I said. "There's no bloke. What about my dad?"

Dad had moved down to London. But he came to visit, every month or so, bringing presents and little treats for me. But it seemed like an age between each visit and I ached to see him.

Nanny Edith took me to see him on the train, too. Back in those days, the only announcements at the station were made over the tannoy, there were no screens. There was nothing visual at all. And so, I was totally responsible for making sure we got on the right train.

Walking into Liverpool Lime Street station for the first time, I was bamboozled by the endless line of platforms, the sea of passengers, the noise and the chaos.

'Where's our train?' Nanny Edith signed, as I looked around helplessly.

My heart was pounding as I strained to hear the announcements over the loud speaker. I wanted to see my dad more than anything, and I knew we couldn't miss the train. I didn't want to let Nanny Edith down either. But this seemed like an impossible challenge. By the time we flopped into our seats, and the guard blew the whistle, I could have cried with relief.

'Well done, darling,' Nanny Edith signed. "I knew I could rely on you."

She understood what an ordeal it had been for me. And of course it must have been a nightmare for her too, but she certainly never showed it. She was a strong, confident little woman and she glided serenely through the station, just as she did through life. Dad met us at the other end, and suddenly all the stress seemed worthwhile as he threw his arms around me.

"I've missed my little girl!" he beamed.

Dad was working as a nurse and he lived in accommodation near the hospital. He showed us his new flat, and then we went into London to see the sights — Buckingham Palace, Trafalgar Square, the Houses of Parliament and Big Ben. Occasionally, we would stay for a few days. It was on one of those trips that I had my first Big Mac Burger, and I thought it was so exotic. There were no McDonalds restaurants in St Helens yet, and this was a totally new experience. As I sat on a bench in Trafalgar Square, swinging my legs and munching on my burger, I felt like I was truly ahead of my time.

"This is the best day out, dad," I told him.

I idolised him still. In his absence, as is often the way, I created an ideal even more wonderful than the reality. He was promoted from wizard to superhero in my child's world. I was desperately loyal to him – or the idea of him – and I hated mum's new fella even before I met him. I didn't ask mum about him. We didn't have those sorts of conversations. And she certainly couldn't be bothered to tell me herself. But suddenly, she was out every night, without any kind of explanation.

I was left as usual to make my own meals, wash my own dishes, tuck myself into bed.

"Mind the ghost," mum would say, as she sprayed on her favourite 'Tweed' perfume, ready for her night out.

"Anyway, how do I look?" she asked.

"Fine," I mumbled.

"Watch out for the ghost," she warned again. "The Middlehurst curse runs through us all, like blood. Be careful, Joanne."

She seemed to cackle, witch-like, at the end of her sentence, but I was irritated, not afraid. I liked to think, even at that young age, that I was one step ahead of her.

Mum was convinced our house was haunted by a little girl, called Judith. One day, she called me into her bedroom, where the word 'Judith' had mysteriously appeared, high on the wall, in blue felt-tip pen.

"Look at that," she gasped theatrically. "The little girl has written her own name on my wall."

But I knew that she was lying. By now, I had come to expect lies from her as standard, and I was as quietly scathing as a small child can be. I was beginning to realise that the Middlehurst Curse was up there with the Tooth

Fairy and the Abominable Snowman. Like I said, I was growing up quickly. And anyway, she hadn't even bothered to disguise her own handwriting.

She would tell me stories too, of the ghost of an Alsatian dog, which apparently also haunted our house.

"I once woke up in the dead of night, and it was there, panting by my bedside, drooling on the carpet," she whispered.

"I was scared, Joanne. I couldn't switch on my lamp, I was so scared."

Again, I was sceptical. Mum knew full well I was terrified of Alsatian dogs, since Nanny Pat's Ben had bitten me. So it seemed a happy coincidence that now we had an Alsatian ghost.

"I'll be OK," I replied.

In some ways, I would rather have faced the ghosts than my mother. I reckoned they probably didn't tell as many lies.

And actually, when mum disappeared out for the night, I quite liked being in the house on my own for a time. I'd play my Madonna records at full blast, especially if I found myself wobbling for a moment and worrying about 'Judith'. I whiled away the evenings, reading magazines or colouring in patterns, until it was bed-time. I would line up cheese and onion crisps on the electric fire, to warm them for my supper. But climbing into bed, the room damp and cold – and so quiet — I'd get a sense of overwhelming loneliness and usually I cried myself to sleep. The puzzle books lay on the sofa, lonely, jilted. And I realised, with a crushing sense of disappointment, that those nights, just the two of us, had simply been a stop-gap for her. She was bored, on her own, and so she had used me as light entertainment. Now she had a new man, and I was surplus to requirements. I had filled a temporary hole in her life. Nothing more. Angry tears stung my eyes. The rejection hurt. But I was more annoyed that I had allowed myself to be taken in by her. I had left myself wide open. I prided myself on being one step ahead of her, only this time, I hadn't been.

Soon after, I celebrated my ninth birthday. Dad sent presents from London and promised to visit soon. And, to my surprise, mum bought me a birthday cake. It was unlike her and I was pleased, grateful even. But it was as though she had to dilute her show of extravagance with some cold reality, and she paid me no more attention for the rest of the day. I disappeared outside to play with my friends, and when mum called me in, I was annoyed.

"Can't I stay out and play?" I whined. "It's my birthday, mum, come on!"

Truth be told, I didn't want to spend an evening with her, watching her drink in front of a mind-numbing series of telly programmes.

"It's my birthday!" I shouted again.

But at this, she ran out into the street, to drag me inside, and I knew my time was up. I ran all the way upstairs and into bed; thoroughly miserable. Later, when I heard mum's footsteps outside my door, I closed my eyes, pretending to be asleep. Whatever it was she had to say, I didn't want to hear it.

But to my surprise, I felt her leaning over me and she placed a gentle kiss on my cheek. I couldn't remember the last time she had kissed me and, after she left my room, I had to blink back confused tears.

It was a single show of affection that I would never forget. But my birthday was soon forgotten and the mystery man, whoever he was, was the new fad. Then one morning, there he was. He had longish, fair hair and though he was only 5'10", he seemed to loom over me, like a threat.

"I'm Karl," he smiled. "Has your mum told you about me?"

He had bought me a Wispa bar but I took it without a word and glared at him suspiciously. And when he turned away, I made a rude face behind his back. I was determined not to like him.

"Not my dad," I muttered, loudly enough so I hoped he would hear.

Those three words were my mantra and I was determined to stick to them. It wasn't easy, because Karl was friendly. He paid me more attention than my mother did. But I hated him even more for that. He wasn't my dad. I wanted nothing to do with this second-rate replacement. I resented him taking what little I had of my mum away from me, too. From the way I saw it, there was no chance now at all of her taking any notice of me. I was bottom of the popularity charts again. The puzzle books, unopened and piled up on the couch, were testament to that.

Whenever Karl asked me to do anything, I would treat him with total contempt.

"You're not my dad," I sneered. "You can't tell me what to do."

Behind his back, I called him names. I took every opportunity to make him feel uncomfortable. In my mind, he was the reason my own daddy couldn't come home.

He was in the way.

But in later years, when I looked back, I would regret my behaviour towards Karl. He was a decent, caring man. He had a Ford Escort, and he was happy to take me wherever I liked. I was secretly impressed. We'd never had a car before, and I felt like Queen Bee sitting in the front seat, fiddling with the radio dial until I found Madonna. We went for days out to Blackpool and to the Lake District. Karl bought me ice-cream and sticks of rock and, to my shame, it choked me even to thank him.

Mum lived day by day, there was never any planning. But when Karl moved in, he did a big weekly shop, and always came home with a little treat for me — a colouring book or maybe a new hair band.

"Do you like it?" he asked, handing me his latest offering.

"S'alright," I mumbled, snatching it and running upstairs.

Karl carried the shopping in on his own and put it all away in the cupboards. I watched, in interest, as he worked away, and mum lay on the couch. I was too young to understand about the way relationships worked, and I couldn't fathom why he was being so nice to her.

"What's in it for him?" I wondered.

And yet, in her own way, she was making an effort. I had noticed she was wearing make-up and she had smartened her clothes up a bit, too. She was very giggly and flirty with Karl which riled me hugely.

"Not my dad," I said quietly, more to myself than them.

And her behaviour towards me changed too, it was as though she was trying to impress Karl. She would talk to me and ask about my day at school. She cooked lovely dinners for us all, and she was chatty and animated. But I noticed she was still knocking back the booze, though perhaps a little less than usual.

"Lovely dinner, Bernadette," Karl smiled, clearing away the plates. "I'll wash if you dry Joanne?"

But I just stared at him as though he was from Mars. Mum slunk back to the couch with her vodka, and I disappeared upstairs. Karl was left to do the lot on his own.

And yet, that didn't seem to put him off. He bought us a colour TV too and, out of his earshot, I whooped for joy. I watched 'Grange Hill' in glorious technicolour after school and it was absolute luxury. I felt Karl didn't deserve me or, more to the point, my awful mother, though of course I could never tell him that.

But it seemed he was determined to give us both a chance, because it wasn't long before mum informed us that she was having a baby. This for me was simply further confirmation that he was muscling in and pushing my dad out.

"I want nothing to do with it," I replied instantly. "I don't want a baby."

"You haven't even seen it, yet," Karl said gently. "You might change your mind."

"I hate it," I said viciously. "And I won't change my mind."

# CHAPTER 4

All through the pregnancy, I kept my distance. Mum didn't seem to enjoy being pregnant, she certainly wasn't excited. Her bump grew and she barely mentioned it. In fact, I couldn't remember her referring to the baby at all, after the initial announcement.

We didn't buy clothes or baby equipment. We didn't choose names. I wasn't a part of it at all. Then again, I wasn't sure she was either.

In November 1981, I woke up one morning and mum was missing. Later that day, she brought my little sister, Catherine, home from hospital. And, despite myself, I dissolved. The first time I saw her, sleeping soundly in a pram in the hallway, I fell in love with her. She became my very own living doll. I would dress her all in white and cuddle her, feed her and take her for walks. By the time Cath, as I knew her, was three weeks old, I was left, aged 10, to look after her alone. One day, I was trying to get a clean nappy out of the drawer, and balancing Cath on the edge of the couch with my other arm. To my horror, she slipped and landed with a bump on the floor. Her lip was bleeding and she started to scream pitifully.

Mum was out somewhere. So I raced upstairs to wake Karl, who was sleeping after a night shift. I ran into the bedroom and pulled at the quilt.

"The front panel fell off the gas fire and hit Cath," I lied. "There was nothing I could do."

Karl didn't question my account. And baby Cath, with just a small bruise, was fine. But I felt a dreadful sense of guilt. Right and wrong, dad had taught me. And this was wrong. I couldn't own up. I just couldn't. But I knew I would never let her down again. And from that moment, I was as fiercely protective as a mother fox with a cub. She became my responsibility. And it was a good job, I used to think, that I loved baby Cath so much. Because my mother certainly didn't seem to make much of a fuss of her. She was too busy arguing with Karl these days.

"Why can't you clean up?" he would ask. "Why can't you cook for us? I'm working all the hours I can. Can't you help?"

"Can't be arsed," was mum's stock reply. "Just can't be arsed."

And the rows just seemed to get worse and worse. Once, as they screamed about money, I saw her go for him with a kitchen knife. Another time, she smashed a lamp over his head and the shards flew everywhere. I would close Cath's bedroom door gently, and sit on the stairs, listening to them screaming, and worrying they would wake her.

Karl had a furious temper and a loud voice. He towered over my tiny mum and his voice boomed from one end of the house to the other.

"God's sake Bernadette!" he bawled. "You've spent the lot again! We've nothing left!"

I used to think, irrationally, that he might kill her. I had seen it was her who triggered the trouble, her who started the violence, time after time and yet, for some reason, I made excuses for her. I would make-believe that it wasn't her fault at all. She was my mother, flawed, failing, desperately wanting in all areas. And yet, she was the only mother I had. And so I lied to myself that it was Karl, not her, who was the aggressor. And I hoped, in time, I might start to believe those lies myself. It was all I could do to keep baby Cath safe, take her from her cot and cradle her in my arms upstairs, listening to the two of them fight it out down below.

"You've got me," I told her. "I'll always look after you. Always."

Soon after Cath was born, Nanny Edith announced she was taking me away on holiday — on a cruise, around the Caribbean, Orlando and Miami. I had never been on a real holiday abroad before in my whole life, and I was torn between the excitement of going away, and the worry of leaving Cath behind.

Nanny Edith bought me new clothes, summer dresses, sunglasses and hats. I was thrilled, but a part of me felt guilty, too. I felt I was letting my baby sister down.

"I won't be long," I promised her sleeping face, as I kissed her goodbye.

She was only a baby, yet I knew she would miss me. I was worried about mum too. It was like I was the parent, leaving two vulnerable children behind. Right up to the last minute, I was hoping some excuse would come up for me not to go.

The cruise was fantastic. On our very first night onboard, Nanny Edith took me downstairs, to an all-night shopping mall, and bought me my very first drink of Dr Pepper. I had never tasted anything so gorgeous.

"This is happiness in a bottle," I grinned, as the bubbles fizzed up my nose.

One day, we docked in Orlando and Nanny took me to Disneyworld. She bought me the biggest ice-cream I had ever seen and I whooped with excitement. But within seconds, there were fat wasps, buzzling angrily around us, and in panic, I threw the ice-cream, uneaten, in the nearest bin. And in that moment, I had a flash of worry for Cath and mum.

"I shouldn't have left them behind," I fretted.

That night, I prayed that they would both be OK. But I had horrible dreams, where I was searching Nanny Pat's house, looking for baby Cath, but I couldn't find her anywhere. And as I pushed open a dark door on the landing, her Alsatian, Ben, suddenly loomed large over me, his jaws dripping with slobber, all over my face and hands. Opening another door, I spotted an orange bedspread and Uncle Bernard, with one solitary eye in the middle of his forehead, lurched towards me, laughing manically. The following morning, I woke up and the sheets were soaking. I had wet the bed.

"Everyone at home will be fine," Nanny Edith signed. "Just enjoy yourself."

I didn't want to disappoint her. She went to such a huge effort on the trip, and I had so many wonderful memories, paddling in clear-blue warm seas, on perfect white beaches. At night, we watched, entranced, as electric storms crackled overhead. But all the same, it was a massive relief to get home and see Cath again. I had missed her more than I thought possible.

"I won't leave you again," I promised, kissing her tiny button nose and putting her soft cheek against mine.

But around us, the chaos and the rows continued. The only saving grace was that mum and Karl didn't see much of each other; Karl worked nights, as a nurse at the local mental institute. Mum was working day shifts as a domestic at the same hospital. Nanny Pat worked there too. Sometimes, mum didn't come home from work at all. She'd just carry straight on to the local pub and stagger home, paralytically drunk, in the early hours of the following day. And when she did come home, she usually had a pack of ale from the off-licence under her arm.

One night, I was woken by groans from downstairs, and I crept down to find mum, grotesque in a black, lacy basque, entangled with a man on the living room floor. He turned to look at me, his mouth hanging open at an angle, his face flushed a blotchy red. I gasped and clamped my hand over my mouth.

"Come here you little bitch!" mum screamed, and she lunged at me.

In terror, I hit out at her and she stumbled, unsteady with drink, and fell backwards. Her head hit the floor with a dull thud. We couldn't afford carpets and as the blood trickled out, over the bare floorboards, my heart did a triple somersault. I thought I had murdered my own mother. In panic, I called Nanny Pat.

"Mummy had an accident," I stuttered, truthful but economical.

Old before my time, my friend had said. Well maybe she was right. I already knew when and how to tell lies.

Nanny Pat sent her friend, Laura, to take me away overnight. She knocked on the door, nodded towards her car, and said: "Get inside. You can stay at my house tonight until this situation calms down."

I spent the night with her but I barely slept. The image of my mum, twisted around a strange naked man, was one I could not forget. But I went back home the next day. I had to. I couldn't leave Cath. Mum, stony-faced, didn't mention the fight. And neither did I.

The weeks passed and there were other men, other tussles. And I just learned to put my pillow over my ears and accept it. Cath was not yet a year old when mum announced she was having another baby.

"What!" I gasped.

My first reaction was one of worry and panic. I already had one baby to look after. I wasn't sure I could cope with another. My heart sank at the thought of it.

Karl and mum were bizarrely ecstatic.

"I hope it's a boy this time," Karl smiled.

"Me too," mum grinned.

I was only 11 years old, but even then I questioned how much forward thinking they had done. Mum clearly didn't like babies. She hadn't looked after me. Or Cath. And I was totally flummoxed as to why she was having another.

But it seemed their wishes had come true, because in December 1982, mum gave birth to a little boy, Chris. He was born prematurely and had to stay in hospital for the first few weeks of his life. When he came home, my worries evaporated. I loved him, just as I had Cath.

Chris suffered with seizures, and so I had to be ready to splash water all over his little face whenever his big, wide eyes started to roll back. I loved looking after him. And the fact that he needed me more seemed to make me love him even more.

"You're my two little cherubs," I would tell them. "My angels."

I adored Cath and Chris. They were my brightness in a dim world. But now, I had double the worry. And double the work.

One day, I came home from school to find baby Chris still in his cot, wearing his baby-gro from the night before. I was on crutches from a sprained ankle and I hobbled around the house, looking for nappies, squealing in pain. Karl was in bed, after working long hours on a night shift. Mum was dozing on the couch.

"We've no nappies, mum," I said.

But she just grunted and refused to even open her eyes. Chris was whimpering in his cot and I couldn't bear to think of him lying in a sodden nappy for a minute longer. In desperation, I found a tea-towel and somehow, I sellotaped it around his legs.

When Karl woke up later, he was horrified. He rushed out for nappies and came back laden with supplies.

"You shouldn't have to do this," he told me, worry etched across his weary face. "I know that you're struggling with the two babies, but I do appreciate your help Joa, I really do.

"What about if I give you some money, would that help?"

I nodded immediately. He offered me £10 a week to take care of the babies and the house.

"Sure!" I beamed, clutching at the note in my hand like it was a golden goose.

That was a lot of money for a young girl and I felt like I'd struck lucky. I was a kid, I only saw what was in front of me, and I didn't understand that in the long run, money would solve nothing at all. And so, at first, I relished my new responsibilities. I'd be up at 7am and make myself a strong coffee before the babies woke up. I'd put a wash on and clean up, and it wasn't long before I heard Cath shouting garbled baby-talk from her cot. With her and Chris tucked up in the double pram, I'd go to the local shop and buy myself a 'Smash Hits' magazine, my secret treat, along with some basic groceries.

We'd come home and have toast and baby rusks, and more often than not, I would sag school and take the kids out to the park.

There was a line of old sheds near the trees. Me and my school mates had found one with a broken latch and filled it with odd bits of furniture, rescued from the rubbish dump.

We even painted a couple of chairs. It looked like a sort of bargain basement Wendy house, but it was nice to take Cath and Chris in there and let them play.

But despite Karl's regular payments, money was always short. Mum would help out occasionally, there were times when she would bring home shopping or pay some bills with her wages. She had worked as a chef when she was younger and she was a good cook, like her own mother. Sometimes she could rustle up a fantastic meal, a stew or a roast dinner. I loved those times. I did my best to compliment her, hoping she would take the hint and cook again.

"It was lovely mum," I told her. "Really nice."

But she never seemed to hear me and it could be months until she cooked again. Most times, she just left me to it. She would pinch Karl's bank card whilst he was asleep and send me to the cashpoint.

"Just get a tenner," she'd say. "I'll manage on that."

Or she'd gather together old jewellery and order me off to the pawn shop. Whatever money I came back with went straight into her purse and, inevitably, straight down to the off-licence.

"We've no nappies for Chris," I told her. "What am I going to do?"

Or: "Cath needs shoes, she's walking now. How will I afford them? How will I even get to the shoe shop on the bus on my own?"

But that wasn't her problem, it was mine. I went to school less and less, because I had my hands full at home. One afternoon, the wag man, Mr Battersby, came and rapped at the door.

"Is your mother in?" he asked.

"She's in bed," I told him.

He insisted that I went up to wake her but, when I did, she swatted me away and refused to come down.

"Tell him I'm not in," she grumbled, pulling the duvet back over her head.

A few days later, a social worker, Miss Lovelady, knocked on our door. This time, she marched in the house herself and right up the stairs to mum's bedroom.

Like a rabbit in the headlights, mum took a new approach.

"I try to get her to school," she lied pitifully. "She won't go. I can't cope with her. I do my best."

The social worker looked from mum to me, waiting for my response, but for some reason, I was silent. Maybe it was shame. Or a misplaced sense of loyalty, or self-preservation. More than anything, it was the fear, in my young mind, of being taken away and separated from Cath and Chris. So I never told anyone what mum was like. I resented her and I despaired of her. But I never hated her. She was another one of my responsibilities. And, curse or blessing, I was, as I had been told over and over, a child who was old before my time. And I took my responsibilities very seriously indeed.

# CHAPTER 5

Just as my young life was looking impossibly bleak, a new girl, Julie Orford, moved onto our street, with her mum, Pat. The first time I spotted her, she was carrying a little pink handbag and wearing jeans with an ultra-fashionable white stripe down the outside.

I knew, just from looking at her, that we'd get on like a house on fire. I could see something of myself in her. A few days later, we bumped into each other on the street and Julie opened her handbag with a cheeky grin.

"Do you fancy a smoke?" she asked, revealing a packet of John Player Superkings and a lighter inside the bag.

I giggled and nodded, even though I didn't, and we disappeared down the entry for a quick fag. Julie swore constantly but, behind the puffs of smoke, she had the kindest face. From that moment, we were best pals. I called for Julie every morning on the days I went to school, and her mum would always insist that I went inside.

"Egg on toast," she said, handing me a plate. "I know you've had no breakfast. Eat up."

She'd make us both a brew as well, before we left the house. She was a no-messing, no back-chat sort of mum, with no money but an endless supply of egg butties and compassion for anyone who knocked on her door. Years later, I would look back and be so grateful for those small kindnesses. They meant a lot to a lonely little girl. After school, we'd take Cath and Chris and the double pram and meet up with our mates. Julie was brilliant; jiggling one baby whilst I cuddled another.

And whilst the babies were in our arms, the double buggy was put to good use. Two of our friends would hop in, another would push, and we would hold time trials, racing round the park. It was a miracle the wheels didn't fall off.

On more than one occasion, a well-meaning passer-by would stop and ask who was in charge of the babies, and why my mother wasn't around.

"She's nipped to the shops," I lied. "She'll be back in a minute. No need to worry."

Again, I didn't really understand why I covered for her. It was a mystery to me, and she certainly didn't appreciate it.

In the evenings, I'd go to Julie's house or she would come around to ours, and after the kids had gone to bed, we'd make a half-hearted stab at some homework together. Or more likely, we'd flick through the latest 'Smash Hits' and learn the words for that week's 'Number One' in the charts.

"Fancy a séance, girls?" mum asked one night. "More fun than maths homework, I bet."

Julie's eyes lit up but inwardly, I groaned. I knew what mum was like. Within minutes, she had scribbled out a home-made Ouija board, with the letters of the alphabet and a 'Yes' and 'No' at either end. Then, she brought two glasses, filling one with lager for herself and turning the other upside down on the coffee table.

She flicked off the light, knelt down onto the floor-boards, and crowed: "Come on girls, link hands and close your eyes. Let's make contact."

Julie and I stifled our sniggers and did as she said. And, as we waited, the glass suddenly slid, quite violently, across the table. It was spooky, but I was not in the least bit spooked. I was determined to see through this and assume the high ground. One of us here needed to be the adult, and it certainly wasn't going to be my mum.

Julie was transfixed, clearly taken in. I made a face at her, trying to show her that mum's knee was firmly wedged under the table.

"She moves the glass herself," I told her later. "She's a crack-pot. You cannot trust a word she says, believe me."

Even as I said it, I felt so disappointed in myself and, more so, in her. Why couldn't she just be a mother? Everyone else seemed to manage it. Why not her?

One night, Julie and I were minding our own business in the living room, when mum laid her home-made Ouija board down in front of us, with her usual mix of drama and reverence.

"One of Karl's friends has died," she told us. "I'm hoping he might come through to me."

I did my usual eye-roll and Julie swallowed a giggle. But we played along, simply because it was easier that way. Anyway, I was always wary of how far I could push mum, I knew what she was and what she could be. And in some ways that made her more sinister.

"Oh, I'm feeling it," she gasped, clutching our hands tightly. "He's coming through. He's coming through."

Her voice trailed off and then suddenly she gave a deathly wail. I opened my eyes and, in the candlelight, mum looked like a cadaver herself, her face twisted and haggard, her hands porcelain-pale. Though I wouldn't admit it, I was unnerved.

"He wants us to go to his house, because there are gold sovereigns hidden in the loft," she cackled. "He wants me to have them. Go girls, now! There's no time to waste!"

She flicked on a lamp and scribbled down an address.

"That's the other side of St Helens," I protested. "It's two buses away and we've got school tomorrow."

"Gold sovereigns," mum repeated. "Go!"

It seemed to me that she had an evil glint in her eyes. I tried telling myself it was probably just the reflection of the light, but I felt horribly uneasy. Either way, I knew this wasn't the right time to argue.

"How will we get in?" I asked feebly. "Did he mention a spare key?"

Mum snorted.

"You'll have to break in, girls," she said shortly. "Don't let me down."

She pushed us towards the front door, me still counting out coppers for our bus fare, Julie a bumbling mess of nerves and giggles.

"Your mum is crazy," she said, as we tumbled out into the street. "Absolutely crackers."

"Tell me something new," I complained.

The bus journey was bizarre; neither of us had any idea why we were going or what we were going to do there. I oscillated violently between hysterical terror and scornful calm. And I couldn't quite make my mind up which it was to be.

When we finally arrived we walked nervously towards the house. It was in darkness and boarded up.

"Well, that's it then," I said, with a perverse logic that even I didn't understand. "We can't break in if it's boarded up."

Julie nodded, her whole body relaxing with relief.

"Never mind," she said, and we crossed over and caught the next bus back. It was all so clear on the bus ride home. There had never been any possibility whatsoever that we would burgle a dead man's house. We had seized upon the first excuse we found. But I was worried how mum would react, when we got home without her gold treasure. Surprisingly, she just threw her hands back in mild annoyance.

"He wanted us to have those sovereigns," she said.

Julie went home and I went to bed and idly wondered whether The Middlehurst Curse would finish my mother off before the booze. It would certainly be a close-run contest.

Not too long after, mum informed me she was making a spell, and that she needed a lily to perfect her mixture.

"It's a potion that will bring you good luck, Joanne," she told me mysteriously. "But first you must dig up a lily – and it must be a lily at all costs – and at midnight.

"No sooner, mind. Or the spell will be ruined."

Part of me was silently ridiculing her. But I had to admit, I was enthralled, too. Julie and I had since laughed so much about the bus ride to the dead man's house, and I thought this might be a bit of a giggle too.

"Ok," I agreed. "I'll do it."

Mum explained she'd seen lilies growing in a garden three blocks down the street. I knew the house, because there was a girl around my age who lived there. I even called for her from time to time but of course I'd never taken stock of her garden. I had never seen the need. The night dragged on and by 11pm my eye-lids were drooping.

"Joanne," mum snapped sharply. "Stay awake! This is important!"

At midnight exactly, she opened the front door and I crept down the street with a large spoon – the nearest thing I could find to a spade! I came to the house with the lilies and, as I pushed the gate, there was a faint, eerie whine. I felt desperately exposed. My heart was thumping loudly. I half expected a spotlight from a police helicopter to light me up at any moment, and an officer with a loud hailer to shout: "Joanne Lee! Game's Up!"

I scrabbled at the earth with my spoon, desperately trying to dig up the lily as quickly as I could. In the end, I panicked and yanked it out, snapping some of the root, unable to stay there a moment longer. I raced up the street, soil flying, with my prize in my hand. I felt like I was running from the law. Once inside, I slammed the door and Mum grabbed it from me and muttered a string of incantations.

"Take it back," she ordered, handing the wilting plant back to me.

I was dropping with exhaustion and confusion, and the only sensible option seemed to be to plant the lily in my own garden. There was no way I could face putting it back where it belonged.

But I would come to regret my decision, because in the months that followed, I could no longer allow our neighbour's daughter into our house, in case she recognised the stolen lily in our garden. My child's mind was sure she would spot it as her own. I spent hours fretting about it, worrying I would be exposed as some sort of horticultural sneak-thief.

And as for the spell, I don't remember any good luck coming my way, or mum's. In fact, it seemed to have quite the opposite effect.

# CHAPTER 6

On our birthdays, and at Christmas, we had presents from various family members. Mum didn't really get into the spirit, unless she was knocking back spirits, but she would put up a tree, begrudgingly. It was a few years before I realised she decorated a Christmas tree only to satisfy Nanny Pat, and for no other reason.

She didn't come to nativity plays or carol concerts and as I grew older, I would tell myself I didn't want her there anyway.

We spent every Christmas Day with Nanny Pat, it was an unwritten rule in the family. Nanny Pat measured out our gifts as though she was working to an exacting recipe. She made sure we got just enough. Enough for the neighbours to nod approval, enough to stop people talking. It was all about keeping everyone else happy – not us. As with every special occasion, her entire, pristine, 'eternal bow' dinner set came out, the table was polished, the children were disciplined.

It was exactly how things should be.

Nobody, not me, my mother, or any of my aunts, dared to disagree. Nanny Pat's selfless present to us all was crippling repression, passed down through each generation.

One year, I'd asked Santa for a sovereign ring. I'd seen one I loved in a local jewellery shop and I had set my little heart on it. All my friends were asking for one too. It was the 'must have' accessory that Christmas.

When I spotted a small jewellery box, neatly wrapped, my heart leapt. Eagerly, I ripped off the wrapping and opened the box. And inside was a little plastic badge, shiny and cheap, which said: 'I've got everything.'

My happiness deflated like a popped balloon and I looked at mum, angry tears glistening in my eyes. But she just shrugged casually. As though she didn't understand the big deal. I bit back the tears, determined not to cry. I wouldn't let her win. No way. I was so used to coping on my own. Relying on nobody. But because it was Christmas, I had got slightly soppy and let my guard down. I had dared to hope. Well, it wouldn't happen again.

It wasn't long after Christmas that I came down in agony with toothache. Mum had never taken us to the dentist, not once. But when I could stand it no longer, I looked up the nearest surgery and went along myself.

"Please take out my tooth," I pleaded. "It hurts so much."

The dentist prodded in my mouth and I yelped in pain.

"It does need to come out," he agreed. "But we can't do it without a parent's consent."

My heart sank.

"Please," I begged. "My mum won't come to the dentist. No chance."

He sighed and went off to talk to the dental nurse. A while later, he came back and smiled.

"Just this once," he said. "Make sure you clean your teeth in future, young lady."

When I got home, my mouth swollen and sore, mum didn't even look up from her magazine. Cath and Chris were playing on the floor, hungry and whining. Wearily, I opened a tin of spaghetti hoops for them and popped some bread in the toaster. Mum lazed on the couch as I fed them, cleared away the dishes, and ran the bath ready for them. It was a miserable existence for two toddlers. But I was a child myself, processing tasks, doing the best I could. My mouth was still throbbing when I tucked them up in bed.

"Good night darlings," I told them. "Sleep tight."

Wearily, I made my way downstairs, wondering if I could manage a cup of tea myself before bed, or whether the pain would be too raw. Then, mum called from the living room.

"Be a good girl and nip to the off-licence for some cigs. There's money in my purse."

I knew better than to argue. My mouth ached all the way to the shop. And my heart raged with the injustice of it all. There was lots wrong with my life. And above all, at the very heart of this, it just wasn't fair. I wanted better for us all. With Karl on nights, mum had free rein to drink and carry on just as she pleased. And she did exactly that. One night, to my horror, she announced she had invited a few of my mates round for a drink.

"What?" I spluttered. "Why would you do that?"

She explained she'd bumped into a few of the lads I knew, outside the shop, and she'd decided to throw a little party.

"You can join in, you can have a few drinks and a smoke," she cajoled. "Come on, what's wrong with you? Loosen up Joanne."

Part of me was tempted. This was every teenager's dream, after all. But of course I wasn't exactly a typical teenager.

"What about Cath and Chris?" I snapped. "Who's going to look after them?"

Mum took no notice, and that evening, as I read Cath 'The Three Little Pigs', I heard a knock at the door. By the time I got downstairs, there were four or five teenage lads gathered in the living room. Mum was splashing lager into Karl's beer glasses and handing them round.

"Does he know about this? Karl?" I said in a loud whisper.

"Ooh, she is so uptight," mum giggled, as she handed out the drinks. But she paused just long enough to shoot me a death stare too. I felt sick inside. She put on her Queen album and soon the house was vibrating with the noise.

"I'll just check on the kids," I mumbled, dashing upstairs.

I was caught in the middle. I didn't want my school-friends to see me sulking and not joining in. But I had responsibilities. I had to think of Cath and Chris. Because if I didn't, who would? Worse still, it was mortifying having to watch my mother simpering like a school girl. She and I had swapped roles. Again, it was dreadfully unfair.

But those nights became a regular thing. And so I just had to get used it.

I would sit and watch, burning with shame, as mum twisted her hair through her fingers, giggling and slurring as she knocked back yet another vodka. She told outlandish stories of how she'd had a fling with the popstar Michael Jackson, and she even claimed that he was Cath's biological father.

I felt myself cringing on her behalf.

"Your mum is brilliant," marvelled my mates. "Wish mine was like that."

"She's nothing like that really," I told them crossly, crimson with shame. "It's a sham."

One night, I saw her swaying in the living room, her glass tipping as she danced, drunkenly, around the furniture.

I could have died of embarrassment.

"Mum, please," I groaned.

One of the lads, Mark, slipped a sympathetic arm around me.

"I don't think she means any harm," he said. "You have to admit; your mum is good fun."

What a pity, I thought, that her sense of good fun didn't extend to her own kids.

"The only fun in our family is in dysfunctional," I told him miserably, and he laughed.

The next day, I was telling Julie all about the party, and she said: "I'm sure Mark fancies you. He never stops talking about you whenever I see him."

"I doubt it," I snorted.

I saw Mark most evenings, at the local park. But I was always pushing a double buggy, too busy with Cath and Chris to really notice him. He was two years older than me as well, which seemed a lot to a teenager.

"No, he does," Julie insisted. "Trust me."

I wanted a boyfriend. Most of my pals wore make-up, bought trendy new clothes and had boyfriends who took them out on a Saturday night. And deep down, I was envious. I felt left behind, when in effect, my life had actually zoomed ahead. I had fast-forwarded through the teenage years, and I was living the lifestyle of a middle-aged mum, weighed down with the worries of children and money and housework. If I was honest, I didn't fancy Mark. But I didn't exactly *mind* him either.

It would be a bit of a laugh, I decided.

That weekend, Julie and me concocted a plan. I went round to see her and she plastered me in her mum's make-up and drenched me in perfume.

"I can't go out like this! I look like a clown!" I gasped, and we both fell about laughing. We had a swig of sherry each from her mum's drinks cabinet and it felt good to be 14 years old. For once, I was just a teenager.

Later, as we strutted down the street, Mark walked past with his mates and whistled.

"You're a bit of alright," he said admiringly. "Come over here!"

Coyly, I sidled over. Mark slipped his arm around my waist and I caught a wink from Julie.

He pulled me into the entry, in-between the terraced houses, and we kissed. My first snog. It moved quickly from there. We began seeing each other every night. One night, at a friend's house, after forcing down half a bottle of brandy, Mark and I did *it* on the living room floor. It was more of a relief, a job well done. I had lost my virginity and I could tick it off the list. I still didn't actually fancy Mark that much if I was honest, but he was an escape, affection, attention.

Now that Mark and I were going out together, I didn't mind mum's parties as much. I got to see him and baby-sit at the same time. He was allowed to stay overnight and again, I was the envy of all my friends.

"Wish my mum was like yours," they all said again.

"You really don't," I replied.

I noticed, in dismay, that Mark was totally taken in by mum's tall stories and her silly behaviour.

"She's a total joke," I said viciously.

"You're too hard on her," Mark replied. "Give her a break."

I couldn't work out how she did it. She seemed to have men eating out of the palm of her hand. Word spread and Karl heard all about her little gatherings. They had horrendous rows.

"You're making a show of us all!" he shouted. "Think of the kids!"

But nothing much changed. Karl worked nights. And Mum carried on just the same as before.

One night, Mark and I went off out to meet some friends and I had such a good time, just being with other teenagers, forgetting about my troubles, that time slipped away. It was a Monday – bingo night for mum and Nanny Pat – and I was needed at home for Cath and Chris.

By the time I realised, it was already past 8pm. Running home, my heart hammering, I was alarmed to find the house in darkness.

Cath and Chris were fast asleep upstairs. No harm done. But I felt dreadful, leaving them at risk, on their own.

"Won't happen again," I promised, kissing their cheeks as they slept.

When mum arrived home, later, she was livid.

"Where were you?" she scolded. "I had to go out and leave Cath and Chris on their own! You should have been here to look after them!"

Suddenly, I felt my temper bubble up.

"Me!" I shrieked. "Whose kids are they? You left them and went to bingo and they're your children! Yours!"

But mum wasn't about to start taking responsibility for anyone, not herself, and certainly not her children. She seemed to genuinely think that she had every right to be angry. She had no concept of what was acceptable – of right and wrong. I wasn't sure whether she was fooling me, or herself, or us both.

"Nanny Pat will hear about this," she said menacingly. "You're for it, Joanne."

"Tell her what you want," I spat, sounding braver than I felt. "They're your children. Not mine. And I'll tell Nanny Pat the same."

I knew I was right. I could hear dad's voice, in my ear, telling me so. But I also knew I was the only one who would lie awake that night, racked with guilt, worrying that I had let my little brother and sister down.

# CHAPTER 7

In January, six months after Mark and I had got together, I missed a period. I felt sure, instinctively, that I was pregnant and I was scared. But by now, at 15, I felt I could cope with most things. I went along to the family planning clinic for a test. I didn't have a coat that winter, so I wore a jacket with big, eighties-style shoulder pads. Somehow, it gave me a bit more confidence as I marched into the clinic. I felt like a real adult with my big shoulders. A nurse did a test, there and then, and the pregnancy was confirmed. I felt a mixture of terror and excitement.

"We need you to come back with your mum," the nurse told me.

Inwardly, I winced. It wasn't, as the nurse suspected, that I was worried about telling mum. I doubted very much that she'd be interested. But it was the fact that I needed her to come to the clinic. I needed her to do something – for me. And that was a tough one.

CHAPTER 7

"Ok," I sighed. "I will see what I can do."

On my way home, I bought mum a two-litre bottle of lager, as a sweetener. I waited, fidgeting, as she drank two-thirds and then I told her.

"Fucking hell," she said. "You'll have to get rid of it. Nanny Pat will go mental."

"Whatever happens, you need to come to the clinic. The nurses know all about it and they said they want to see you," I persisted.

Mum wasn't happy, but she came.

"You're having an abortion," she told me. "And that's that."

I waited patiently until she had finished making the arrangements for the termination with the clinic staff.

And then, I said "I'm keeping this baby. I'm not having an abortion."

I folded my arms, set my jaw, and that was that. Mum knew she was beaten but she went mad, all the way home. She screamed at me that I was stupid and selfish. She dragged me round to see Nanny Pat and she, in turn, went madder than mad.

"The shame!" Nanny Pat screeched. "The absolute shame!"

I stood obediently whilst they both yelled and wailed over my head, clumps of spittle flying from their mouths and landing in my hair.

But I had made up my mind. Mark came round and blanched when I broke the news. But he did his best to be grown-up.

"We'll cope," he smiled. "Don't worry."

We went to see his family, and his mum, Jean, was lovely to me. Her kindness gave me a little lift.

"We'll look after you and the baby, Joanne," she promised warmly.

She gave me a hug and she rested a hand on my tiny bump. Just as a mum should be, I thought.

I started to feel excited. But deep down, I had a gnawing worry about facing my dad. I knew how disappointed, how saddened, he would be. And that was worse than any fury. In my bedroom, on my own, I played Madonna's 'Pappa don't Preach' over and over. It was as though she'd written it just for me.

Those first weeks of the pregnancy were exhausting and, as soon as the children were asleep, I'd collapse into bed myself. Mark stayed most nights, but he'd drink and joke with mum downstairs until the early hours. He was a big Queen fan and mum knew it. She'd regale him with ridiculous stories of how, as a child, she used to have ballet lessons with Freddie Mercury. I watched, squirming, as Mark drank in every preposterous word she said.

"I've found a new drinking buddy," she told me with a smile. "Mark's a real gem."

It was all I could do not to slap her. It was me who had to clear up the ash-trays and the beer cans the following morning. Me who made breakfast and got Cath and Chris ready for nursery school. I would gag over the smell of smoke and booze as I filled the bin. But mum didn't even get out of bed.

Twelve weeks into the pregnancy, I woke in the night to find Mark's side of the bed empty. I could hear giggling and, creeping downstairs, I pushed open the living room door just a fraction and froze in shock. Mum and Mark, who was 17 by now, were entwined, partially clothed, on the couch. I stepped back, my knees buckling, my heart pounding so loudly I felt sure it would give me away. But they were oblivious. I hid amongst the coats and umbrellas, in the hallway. And that, for three, long, hours, was where I stayed. Disguised as a coat, I listened, rigid, to them laughing and whispering, moaning and sighing. It was toxic. Yet I couldn't tear myself away. I was rooted to the spot in shock. When, eventually, it all went quiet, I peered through the door again and they were fast asleep, in each other's arms. The sight made me nauseous. I checked my watch and realised Karl would be home soon, from his night-shift.

"Let him find them," I thought grimly. "Let him sort her out."

The tears flowed as I climbed back into bed. I didn't sleep at all. Here I was, 15 and pregnant, and now this. The front door banged, and I heard Karl clanking about in the kitchen. I had no idea if he'd seen them on the couch. I strained to listen. But there was no fuss, no argument.

Soon after, Cath toddled in and said: "Mummy said why aren't you up? You need to take me to school."

Unkindly, I turned my back on her and said: "Tell her to take you."

I knew it wasn't poor Cath's fault. But I'd had as much as I could take. Mum thundered in next, and I spat "They're your fucking kids, you take them! I saw you last night. I saw you with Mark! You're supposed to be my mother!"

Mum tilted her head a little.

"I don't know what you're on about," she lied.

I rolled over in bed, my hands around my baby bump, and sobbed. That same day, Karl packed his bags and left. I had been sorry to see him arrive. But it was much worse to see him leave.

# CHAPTER 8

Twisted with fury, I found myself blaming mum – and not Mark. I knew exactly what she was like. Mark was a 17-year-old lad. Easily led and easily laid.

"I'm sorry," he told me. "I was drunk. Give me another chance."

I didn't want to lose him. We had a baby on the way, a future together. And so, I forgave him. I was still smarting, terribly. But I didn't really see any other choice.

Without Karl, we had no money, no routine, no stability. Mum slumped into drinking even more heavily and within weeks she lost her job. She was out every night, often all night. And I was left with the children full-time. If I had thought life was tough before, then this was an eye-opener. The washing machine broke and there was no money to fix it. There was no money left, even for basics like bread, milk and toilet rolls. Instead, I would wait until we ran out of everything and then scavenge the house for change, hoping mum might have left a stray fiver in her coat pocket in a drunken stupor. Early in the mornings, I sent Chris out to steal milk from strangers' doorsteps.

"We're borrowing it," I told him. "Nobody minds, well, not really."

He scooted around the street, grabbing the odd bottle, and stuffing it under his jacket. It was a game to him, he had no idea it was theft.

"The neighbours have all seen Chris stealing milk," Julie's mum told me one day. "You need to have a word with your mum. It's not right. He's going to get into trouble."

Numbly, I nodded. I could have confided in her and told her exactly what was happening at home. But I said nothing. And we limped on.

At school, I nicked tiny bars of soap from the toilets, slipping them into my pockets before any of the other girls saw me. I would have been a laughing stock if they knew we were using school soaps to wash ourselves. I even used them to wash clothes in the bath, rubbing up a lather and scrubbing at clothes, until my fingers were raw and bleeding. At weekends, when I visited Nanny Edith, I would steal the 20 pence pieces from the tin she kept on her fireplace. I felt wretched as I snatched at the money and dropped it into my backpack. Again, it was the wrong thing, for the right reasons. She must have known. But she let it pass. On my way home, I would buy tins of beans, cereal, toilet rolls. Somehow, we coped. But then, our electric was disconnected, followed by the gas and then the water. As soon as we scrimped together enough to get one reconnected, another was cut off. I just couldn't keep up.

Then, came a knock at the door.

"It's a policeman!" Cath gasped, peering from behind the curtain.

Sighing with annoyance, mum went to the door, and I followed.

"We've had a report that your daughter has been having under-age sex," said an officer. "We need to investigate."

"I have not," I lied brazenly. "You're wrong."

They insisted on doing a pregnancy test. I cursed, realising that Karl, no doubt thinking it was for the best, had reported me and Mark. I was only 15, after all. It was arranged that I would take a urine sample into the doctor, and the investigation would go from there.

As soon as they'd left, I turned to mum.

"You owe me," I said meaningfully. "I kept my mouth shut for you. Will you do the urine sample for me? Please?"

It galled me to ask her but I had no choice. To my surprise, she agreed. She presented me with a little pot the next morning, and I skipped off to the doctor's surgery feeling very pleased with myself. Later that day, we had a call from the doctor.

"It's positive," he said. "You're pregnant."

My mind was reeling. What had mum done? Was this some sort of cruel trick? But when I saw her face, sapped of colour, I knew that the joke was on both of us. She'd had no idea she was pregnant. Until now. I didn't dare ask her who the father was – or what she planned to do.

Now, there were social workers and police officers swarming in and out of our lives. There was talk of me going into care.

"No child in this family will go into care," Nanny Pat barked. "Over my dead body."

She was worried, I knew, about the neighbours and the local priest and what they would all think. And how it would look for her. I didn't really figure in her thoughts at all.

Nanny Edith offered to take me. But because she and Grandad were deaf, it was decided I would be able to sneak out, unnoticed, to meet Mark. And so their home was ruled to be unsuitable.

"You're coming with me," Nanny Pat boomed. "And that's that."

I was distraught.

"What about Cath and Chris?" I sobbed. "Who will look after them?"

I felt like I was walking out on them. Abandoning them both. My mind went back to that moment when, as a baby, I had dropped Cath and blamed my own clumsiness on the fireplace. I had promised her then, faithfully, that I would always protect her.

Now, I was being taken away.

"You can visit," Nanny Pat agreed stiffly. "We'll pop in when we can."

She knew, as well as I did, what mum was like. Of course neither of us actually voiced it. The veil of secrecy that was stretched tight across our whole family made me want to scream. Nanny Pat drove me home in aggrieved silence, as if the burden was all hers. When we arrived, she pulled on the handbrake and turned sharply to where I was slumped, desolate, on the back seat.

"You will behave yourself here," she said fiercely. "There will be none of that under my roof. You will not be allowed out and you will not see that boy."

She didn't mention the baby. But then, her denial was no less than I would have expected. A teenage pregnancy didn't sit well with the Victorian values and the stinking hypocrisy that she lived her life by. I was thoroughly miserable, worried about Cath and Chris, concerned for my own future too, with my baby. Would they let me keep it? I felt a flutter inside me, and it felt as though my baby, at least, was on my side.

# CHAPTER 9

She lived only five miles away. But that first night, in Nanny Pat's spare bedroom, I felt so far away, I might as well have been on the moon. My aunts by now had left home and the room was quiet and eerie. As I climbed into bed, the sheets were clean but cold and stiff; exactly the sort of hospitality I'd expect from Nanny Pat. I thought of Cath and Chris, tucking themselves into bed, all alone, wondering in their childish innocence why I had deserted them. The tears flowed down my cheeks. Whatever mess we were in, we had always been in it together. Without them, I felt lost. I was unsettled too, Nanny Pat's house scared me, especially in the dark. The house was large, with high, lofty ceilings. And yet I felt suffocated. Trapped. At the end of the hallway was the dark box room, Uncle Bernard's room, and now, I convinced myself in the half-light, it was where the Bogeyman lived. Every so often, a breeze rattled down the hall from the bathroom window, and the door of the box room creaked and groaned with a bronchial wheeze. I caught sight of the orange bedspread and a shiver ran through me. I must have dozed off eventually, only to be startled by the sound of Nanny Pat cracking a metaphorical whip over my bed.

"School!" she shouted. "We will start as we mean to go on."

That same afternoon, I was sitting in Geography class on the third floor, struggling to stay awake. And suddenly, out of the window, I spotted Dad marching up the path towards the school office.

"Oh God," I breathed. "No."

I realised the police must have called him. I felt a crushing sense of failure, so acute I could barely breathe. I had let him down. And I had to face him. Minutes later, the headmistress marched into the lesson and took me out.

"You're coming with me," dad said firmly.

By now, he was living in Devon, and we drove all the way along the motorway in silence. We arrived at his new house and I sat sullenly in the spare bedroom. The days passed. And I didn't say a word.

"You need to speak to me, Joanne," he pleaded. "We need to sort this out. You're not old enough to have a baby."

But by now, my thoughts had moved on from my pregnancy. With me in Devon, Cath and Chris were left completely alone – with mum. I had to get back to them. I was worried sick.

"If you won't talk, I might as well take you home," dad decided. "This has been a wasted journey."

I was so relieved. That was exactly what I wanted.

Dad drove me back to St Helens, and back to Nanny Pat.

"Can I see Cath and Chris?" I asked anxiously. "I'll get the bus. I don't mind."

It was too far to slip out unnoticed. I needed permission. Nanny Pat pursed her lips and said, "Maybe later."

That night, in May 1987, she agreed to take me to mum's house. When I arrived, I threw my arms around 5-year-old little Cath and breathed in the smell of her hair.

"Missed you, Joa," she lisped.

"Me too," I said.

I was so pleased to see her, and Chris too. But, while we chatted and played, I felt a horrible, dull ache in the bottom of my stomach.

"I'm going up to run a bath for you two," I said.

As I switched the taps on, I heard a muffled giggle, and turned to see Mark standing in the bathroom, hiding behind the door.

"Your mum phoned me and told me you were coming," he whispered. "But she told me to hide up here, away from Pat."

"Great!" I whispered.

Much later, I would look back on my own naivety in exasperation. It was very unlikely that mum had called Mark, on my behalf, and much more probable that he was there to see her – not me.

But in that moment, I either couldn't, or wouldn't, see the truth of it. I wrapped my arms around him, my face in his neck, and the feel of his strong arms around me was so reassuring. Nanny Pat was just a few feet away, downstairs. We were living dangerously. But that just made it all the more exciting. Cath and Chris trundled upstairs and Mark disappeared back into a bedroom. The kids splashed in the bath and chattered endlessly, and I felt so glad to see them again. But, as I leaned over with a towel, I suddenly felt a twinge of pain.

"Maybe this is just what happens," I said to myself.

After all, I had no idea what it was like to be pregnant. And there was nobody for me to confide in. Nanny Pat drove me home and I began to feel tired and sickly. Nobody noticed when I disappeared off to bed for an early night. But later, with the house in darkness, I woke in agony. Stumbling to the toilet, I could feel something wedged between my legs. In my ignorance, I tried to push it back with my finger. Then, I staggered back into my bedroom and banged on the wall which adjoined Nanny Pat's room. She marched into the room like a sergeant major, threw back the bed covers and looked me up and down like I was part of a kit inspection.

"I've got awful stomach ache," I moaned. "I think it's the baby."

"Take two paracetamol and go to sleep," she rapped. "Don't fuss girl. Don't fuss."

She spoke in the same clipped rhythm made by her Scholl shoes on the wooden floor, and her tone was icy with disinterest. As she left the room she turned and stared at me, without saying anything. She knew how to frighten a child and I didn't dare shout again. I was too scared even to go to the bathroom, because Ben, the Alsatian, had positioned himself on the landing, jaws heavy with drool, one eye half open. Soon, I was in too much pain to leave the room anyway. I crawled around the bedroom floor on all fours, desperate to ease the cramps. By now, I was bleeding heavily, all over the floor and the bed-sheets.

By 9am, there was movement in the house.

"Surely, someone will come," I thought. "Surely someone cares."

But I could smell toast and hear voices chatting. It seemed as though they had forgotten about me. I couldn't help screaming as another wave of agony swallowed me whole, and Grandad Bernard poked his head around the door to investigate.

"Pat!" he shouted. "You had better come and look at this."

She was in the kitchen, and as she click-clacked her way towards me, I felt a sense of relief that at last help was coming.

But Nanny Pat took a cursory look at my white face and the blood-stained sheets and said: "I'll call the doctor later."

And then, she was gone.

The hours dragged and I slipped in and out of consciousness. Sometimes, I was barely aware of whether I was alive or dead, or if there was even much of a difference between the two.

Eventually – it could have been hours, days, weeks later, I was aware of a figure looming over me. The doctor took one look at me and turned to Nanny Pat, his face crimson with anger.

"Call yourself a nursing officer?" he shouted. "Get an ambulance now!"

All around me, there was suddenly chaos and panic. My Uncle Peter, by now a trainee priest, was dispatched to go and bring my mother. Nanny Pat attempted to sit me up and change my blood-stained nightie, ready for the paramedics. It wouldn't do, of course, for them to see what a state she had left me in. Not at all. By the time the sirens sounded, I was already fading into sleep again. But even as I was carried down the stairs, I was dimly aware of Nanny Pat, scurrying outside before us and scanning the street, to make sure that none of the neighbours could see me on the stretcher.

When I came round I was in a hospital room, with Mum, Peter, and Nanny Pat, all standing at one end.

"Catherine and Christopher weren't even at school," Peter was telling Nanny Pat in a disapproving tone. "So I took them myself."

I allowed myself a small sigh of satisfaction that they were at least being looked after, before a wave of pain and nausea engulfed me. Mum's face swam and bobbed in my line of vision.

"You're in labour, Joanne," she told me. "The baby is coming."

I knew it was too soon. But it was also too late.

At 2.50pm, on May 8 1987, my baby boy was laid gently in my arms, and I wept tears of grief and joy. As I gazed at him, I was filled with a love so fierce, so powerful, that it scared me. I knew I would die for this little man. I woozed in and out of consciousness and as I woke, he took his last breath, and with it, the light went out of the world.

He had lived, a nurse told me, for just 30 minutes. He died at 3.20pm.

"I baptised him and I named him John," Peter told me gently. "I know it's your grandfather's name."

I nodded, my soul splintered and smashed with grief. I felt so empty. Mark's mum came and showed me the tiny bootees she had been knitting. We both sobbed together. And it was a comfort to know that she had loved him, too. I wanted him to be mourned. I wanted the whole world to weep. Mark came too, after a tip-off from Julie, upset but angry that nobody had let him know about the birth.

"He's my son," he complained. "Why wasn't I told?"

I could only shrug.

"When's the funeral?" he asked. "I want to go."

Again, I shrugged helplessly. One thing was sure, I would have no say in it at all. I was John's mother. But I would have no say. I felt myself drifting once more. And the next time I came to, I could hear the Eurovision Song Contest blasting out somewhere in the hospital. It seemed so insensitive. My John had deserved better. So much better. The next morning I was allowed to go home, but I refused to leave without seeing my son first. Nanny Pat was livid. She wasn't used to disobedience. But the way I saw it, I had nothing to lose any more.

"I won't leave this place until I say goodbye to John," I said.

She must have sensed the steel in my voice, because eventually I was taken to the hospital morgue. And there he lay, the tiniest and most perfect little angel. He was wearing a minute little crocheted bonnet and was wrapped in a white shawl. His skin was like wax, slightly transparent and heart-wrenchingly pale. He looked just like he was asleep.

"I love you," I murmured. "My son."

I left the morgue sobbing, hardly able to believe I had produced something so wonderful, yet had it taken away from me so brutally.

As I packed my few things into a carrier bag, a nurse came and pressed into my hand a small polaroid photograph of John. He was lying on a hospital paper hand towel, and he wasn't even long enough to reach the end.

Blinded by tears, I muttered a thank you. It was a photo I would cherish.

Then, I was sent home to Nanny Pat's, and she didn't refer to the birth or to my son in any way. I had given birth wearing a pale blue nightie, with green flowers on it. Afterwards, I rinsed the blood out, and folded it safely away. I knew I could never wear it again. But I could never throw it away.

Later that day, I was allowed to visit Cath and Chris and I fell on them with kisses and tears. They were all I had. And I needed them as much as they needed me. The following Thursday, a car arrived outside, and John's tiny white coffin was balanced on the passenger seat. Choked with grief, I wanted to throw my arms around the coffin and whisper my goodbyes. But I had to go in a separate car, with Nanny Pat and mum. There was no service. No flowers. All expenses spared. It was the bargain basement of burials. Instead, we drove straight to the cemetery where Peter said a few prayers at a family grave where my great-grandfather was buried. It was a dismal, overcast day and the sky hung heavy with misery. The whole funeral was over in a matter of minutes. No fuss; it was the family way. As the tiny coffin was lowered into the grave, I had a compulsion to throw myself after it, to go with him, wherever he was going. Because it had to be better than what I had here. Back at Nanny Pat's, nobody mentioned my son again. Nobody even said his name. It was as if he had never existed. As long as there was a crisp, clean tablecloth on the dining table, all was right with the world.

# CHAPTER 10

I went back to school and that was that. But beneath the surface was a simmering hatred, a resentment of Nanny Pat, for what she had done, or not done. It never showed, but it grew and it grew.

It was decided that Pat's mother, my great-grandmother, Winnie, would move in with my mum, to keep an eye on things.

But most days, after school, I would nip back to see Cath and Chris. I helped with their homework, did a batch of hand-washing, made sure they were fed and clean. But each time, leaving them, I felt a dreadful, choking sense of responsibility and guilt. I was neither a child nor an adult. I had been carted off to my grandmother's, to keep me away from an unsuitable boyfriend. And yet every chance I had, I was running home, like a surrogate mother, to look after my siblings. It was an odd time and it was no wonder I was in an odd state of mind. And yet, with that same sense of independence and maturity I'd shown on my first day of school, I managed to keep juggling the two worlds.

"You will look after us, won't you?" Cath asked me anxiously.

And seeing her big hazel eyes, staring at me, pools of worry and uncertainty, was all I needed to keep me going.

"I won't let you down," I told her.

There was very little either of us could rely on. But we had each other. And our bond was bomb proof.

A couple of months on, I was allowed to visit Nanny Edith for the weekend.

"How are you?" she signed. "How are you coping?"

She was the first person to ask me how I was and her kindness, simple as it was, touched my heart. She gave me money too, to pay for John's name to be engraved on the headstone.

"Give this to Pat," she signed. "It's the least I can do."

I handed the money over to Nanny Pat, but I knew nothing would be done. Inscribing John's name on the headstone would be admitting that he had existed.

"And what would the neighbours say?" I thought bitterly.

In years to come, Nanny Edith would ask me to take her to John's grave, but I was too ashamed to tell her about the headstone. And so instead, I lied, and told her I had forgotten where it was.

"It's a big graveyard," I mumbled. "I just can't remember."

It was a silly excuse and we both knew it. John's birth, his death, his grave, were engraved upon my heart.

The weeks passed and my grief threatened to envelop me at times. Mark recovered much more quickly than me, and often he didn't want to talk about John. Despite Nanny Pat's best efforts to keep us apart, he would cycle up to the school gates at lunchtimes to meet me. Sometimes mum would hide him upstairs so that we could snatch a few moments together when Nanny Pat took me to visit. It wasn't much. But I looked forward to seeing him. Now, he was my link to John, and I treasured that.

In November, six months after John's death, Winnie died and was buried in the same grave. Nanny Pat was deeply affected by the loss of her mother and her own health deteriorated. Nanny Pat had always had a heart condition and now it got worse. I saw this as my chance. She was so distracted that she hardly noticed what I was doing. Little by little, I began moving back home – and moving Mark in.

One afternoon, I had sneaked home on the bus after school, and when I arrived, Cath, who was now six, was outside playing in the street, on Chris's red bike.

"That bike is far too small for you," I smiled.

I noticed, with a stab, that she hadn't had her face washed, her hair was tangled and she wasn't wearing her school uniform.

"Where's mum?" I asked.

"In bed," Cath replied. "All day."

Angrily, I marched into the house, past Chris, still in his pyjamas and glued to a cartoon, and stamped upstairs to find her.

"What's going on?" I began. "Why haven't the kids been to school? Again?"

But as I opened the bedroom door, I noticed a large circular blood stain on the dirty cream carpet.

"What's that?" I asked.

Mum was lying face-down on top of the duvet, wearing a vivid green tracksuit.

"Nosebleed," she mumbled into the pillow. "I'm not well."

It was a huge stain, for a nosebleed. The carpet didn't quite fit the room and the stain had leaked onto the floorboards, too. There was a damp, fusty smell. My first thought was that she had slit her wrists. I walked over to the bed and rolled her over, like a great sausage. But there were no marks on her arms.

"That's not a nosebleed," I said sceptically. "There's loads of blood."

I was a little concerned. And then I realised she was sober. Usually she stank of booze. But not today. And now, I was even more concerned.

"Are you alright?" I asked.

I went downstairs to make her a coffee. I couldn't make sense of it. There was far too much blood for it to be a nosebleed. Yet there were no signs of any injuries.

What else could it be?

Mum came downstairs and watched *Blockbuster* on TV and seemed to be her usual self. I was soon busy playing with Cath and Chris, and I didn't think much more about it. I was so used to mum telling me lies by now that I neither believed or disbelieved her. Even so, I was unsettled by the ghoulish stain, and the stagnant smell. That night, I slept at home because I was worried about Cath and Chris. I would take whatever punishment Nanny Pat saw fit. But to my surprise and delight, she didn't seem to care where I was. This was my green light, and by Christmas, I was living back at home full-time, looking after Cath and Chris, running the house and sleeping with Mark. And of course I had to make sure I attended school, as much as I could, to keep the social workers off my back. The last thing I wanted was a court order sending me back to Nanny Pat's. A small piece of me missed having clean sheets, ironed clothes and a hot meal every night. But my place was here, with my sister and brother. And despite the miserable state of the house, I was so glad to be home.

By now I was 16. But the ordeal of losing John had aged me immeasurably. As a mum myself, I looked on my own mother through fresh eyes, with disgust and amazement. I knew how precious it was to hold your baby in your arms. Yet she threw that privilege back at her children, every single day of their lives. So now, when she went out boozing, leaving us without food or heating, I challenged her.

"Step up and be a mother!" I told her. "You're a disgrace!"

Mum gave as good as she got, especially after a few drinks. Our arguments became physical and we had many a fist fight, rolling around the living room. I had so much anger and frustration bubbling inside, and it felt good to unload just a small amount.

I never asked her what had happened with her own pregnancy. I presumed she had maybe suffered an early miscarriage. I was so clouded, so swamped by the loss of my own baby, that I had no tears left for hers.

# CHAPTER 11

As the weeks passed, the pain of losing John only seemed to intensify. And I became determined to have another baby. At first, it was an anxiety, a longing, to be a mum again. But then, it became almost obsessive.

"I will have a baby and nobody will take this one away from me," I would tell myself.

It wasn't that I could, or would, replace John. His place in my heart was secure forever. But now that I had felt that overwhelming, earth-shattering devotion, that comes from holding your own baby in your arms, I became desperate to feel it again.

"Let's try for a baby," I pleaded with Mark.

He was working by now, as a labourer, and I was due to leave school in a few months. In my mind, I was already an adult. To me, I was ready. Mark agreed but of course neither of us had any real idea of what lay in store. I had noticed too, the knowing looks and flirtatious smiles he and mum shared. He was closer to her than I ever would be. It was a knife through my heart, every time I caught them giggling together. If I had been as grown-up and wise as I thought I was, I would have realised that having a baby with Mark was absolutely the last thing I should have been doing. But I was a daft teenager, and even after my topsy-turvy childhood, I had a lot to learn. I harboured stupid hopes that a baby would bring us together – and push mum out.

Sure enough, in March 1988, I missed a period. When my pregnancy test was positive, I was over the moon. This time, I decided, I would tell nobody except Mark and Julie. I didn't want to tempt fate. And I certainly didn't want to give Nanny Pat the chance to take this baby away too. This time, I was determined to do everything right. I went to every ante-natal appointment. When Mark couldn't come with me, Julie came instead. After my 12-week scan, I went home to face mum.

"I'm pregnant," I told her. "And I'm keeping the baby."

She didn't seem too fussed. I knew I could rely on her not to tell her own mother, not because of any sense of loyalty to me, but rather because she was terrified of Nanny Pat's reaction, or over-reaction, as it surely would be. I was gripped by a mixture of anxiety and excitement as my bump grew and I felt the first flutters of movement in my stomach. Some days, when my baby kicked, I was bursting with happiness. I applied for benefits and spent every penny I had on a pram, a cot and a car seat. Mark's mum bought baby clothes and was constantly knitting tiny jackets and bootees. After losing John, she, like me, was desperate to hold a baby in her arms.

"You're putting on weight," Nanny Pat remarked sharply, eyeing my stomach when she visited.

I shrugged.

"I can't help it," I replied casually. "Mum's the same. Must run in the family. Like a curse, you know."

It was true, mum did gain and lose weight easily. She was a life-long yo-yo dieter. I hid behind that smoke screen and, under baggy jumpers and tracksuit bottoms, my bump grew. Most of the time, I managed to avoid Nanny Pat and her critical eye. If she was calling round, I'd make sure I went out. And I was no longer so in awe of her either, not since losing John. Grief had made me fearless.

One afternoon, Cath and Chris were playing outside when suddenly there was a blood curdling scream from the garden. Mum didn't react. I dashed outside, to find Chris had accidentally dropped a paving slab on Cath's foot. She was hysterical.

Bending was difficult, with my baby bump, but I managed to lift the stone off, and examine her foot, which was swelling even as I looked at it.

"Mum!" I panted, running back inside. "Cath needs to go to hospital. Look at her foot!"

"Oh, she'll be alright," mum drawled. "I'm not taking her to hospital."

It was what I had expected from her but I was furious all the same. I had no choice but to scoop Cath up into my arms and take her to Whiston Hospital. She was in agony – and so was I. In casualty, the doctors inserted a hot pin through her toe-nail, to release the pressure, and the swelling subsided. We were eventually allowed to go home.

"I can't walk," Cath whined.

But I knew there was no way I could carry her. My bump was already low-slung and felt heavier than usual. I had enough loose change in my pocket to buy her a Twix, and so I bribed her, with the promise of a treat at the all-night garage, to walk all the way home. When we finally arrived at the front door, both of us crying tears of self-pity, mum had gone out.

In that last month, my bump grew huge, and on my regular weekend visits Nanny Edith became more and more suspicious.

"Are you sure you're not pregnant?" she signed.

But I shook my head. Nanny Edith had always been kindness itself. But for some reason, I couldn't tell her. Thinking I was piling on the pounds, she bought me an exercise bike, which was set up in her spare bedroom upstairs. Every weekend, when I visited, I would spend an hour or so in the bedroom, sitting on the floor and idly turning the pedals with my hands, to keep the pretence going.

But by December, I was 40 weeks gone, and I felt I could lie no longer.

"Are you pregnant?" she signed again.

"Yes," I replied. "Due last week!"

Nanny Edith put her arms around me.

"Don't worry," she signed. "It will be fine this time."

# CHAPTER 12

Early one morning, in December 1988, I woke with awful stomach pains. I staggered to the toilet downstairs. Mum was asleep on the couch and my groans must have woken her.

"You're in labour," she said, as she watched me doubled over, gripping onto the bathroom door for support.

"Wait here," she continued. "I'll go and call an ambulance."

I was amazed, as she slipped on her coat and went to the phone box on the street corner. I couldn't remember the last time she had done anything for me and I was touched and grateful. By 6.30am, I was on the labour ward, with Mark by my side. Five hours later, our daughter, Natalie was born. Our little girl weighed 6lbs 11ozs and she was so beautiful, it almost hurt me to look at her. Of course the reminders of John were everywhere. This was the same hospital where he had lived and died. And Natalie looked like him too, they shared the same facial features, though she was much bigger. Mum came later in the day, with a tiny dress for her granddaughter. She brought Cath, who had stayed off school, and together they cooed over the cot side.

"I love her," Cath told me, her eyes shining.

She had a cuddle, and then mum took a turn too. But it was as if she was fulfilling a task; she held Natalie as though she was a parcel, before plonking her back in the cot.

Bringing my baby home was the proudest day of my life. And I adored being a mum. Of course, I had done it all before, changing nappies, washing baby clothes, sterilising bottles. But doing it for my own baby was different. It was the highest honour I could have wished for.

I was rushed off my feet now though. I had Cath and Chris to look after too. It was hard work, rushing out on the school-run with a tiny baby. Grandad John had recently suffered a stroke, so I would visit my grandparents, every day, to help out. And now, even with my benefits, we had to make the money go further. We seemed to lurch from day to day, from one crisis to the next. Mum lay in bed, like a great, lazy, sweaty lizard, glued to her latest gruesome magazine. She would order monthly true-crime series from the newsagent and she loved murder stories the best. Either those, or horror stories. I didn't even bother asking her for help. I knew I was wasting my breath.

Cath came home one day excitedly carrying a letter with details of a school trip to Wales.

"Can I go?" she asked.

I shook my head sadly. We had no money for the basics, never mind the extras. There were no new clothes, no trips, no treats. Nanny Pat had a friend who owned a caravan in the Lake District and Cath and Chris had been once or twice, overnight. It was the closest thing they'd ever had to a holiday. There were neighbours on our close who felt sorry for them, who would give them a bag of crisps or a bottle of pop when they saw them out playing. Julie's mum was always kind. And Karl did his best. He made many an arrangement to come and see his children. But when he knocked on the door, mum would order us all to be quiet so he thought nobody was at home. It wasn't that she didn't want him to see them. Her worry was that he would go mad at the state of them — their dirty clothes and their knotted hair. She couldn't be bothered to get them ready, couldn't face brushing their hair and so she simply ignored the door. Cath and Chris thought it was funny at first, they would laugh as we lay motionless on the floor, curtains drawn, while Karl rapped on the doors and windows. But as time went on, they missed their dad. They missed having fun.

"You're not being fair," I told mum.

But she didn't seem to listen. One day, there was a knock at the door and my aunt Dish was waiting.

"Your Nanny Pat wants to see you and the baby," she told me. "Hop in the car."

When we arrived, Nanny Pat met me in the hallway and glared.

"I should have nothing more to do with you," she said sternly. "But since you're here, you had better come in."

To my amazement, she seemed to melt as she lifted Natalie out of her car seat.

"She's beautiful," she told me approvingly. "And so clean. So well turned out. She's a credit to you."

I went home that afternoon reeling from the shock of the first compliment I'd ever had from Nanny Pat. Mum seemed to take more of an interest in Natalie too. She fussed over her more than she ever had over me, and I was glad. Her maternal instinct had obviously skipped a generation, like some sort of defective gene. But just before Christmas, as life was looking up a little, the gas was disconnected again.

"Great timing," I groaned.

Next, the electric went off.

It could – should – have been a disaster. But we had become remarkably resilient. I visited Nanny Edith and without asking me to explain, she showed me a stack of camping gear in her garage. I took home a battery-operated light and a camping stove.

"It's exciting!" Cath beamed.

Each night, I hung the light upstairs, until she and Chris were asleep. Mum and I had to sit downstairs in the dark, without a TV or radio. In-between our miserable scraps of conversation, I could hear the sound of her popping open new cans of lager. There was always money for lager. Always. A few days later, she got one of her pals to put our electric on the fiddle, and hey presto, there was light. We felt like royalty, basking in the brightness of the fluorescent strip in the kitchen. It was luxurious – decadent to the point of vulgarity – just to plug in an electric fire.

Before school, Cath and Chris made toast on the electric bars. It was like an outdoors adventure for them.

"Can we sleep outside tonight?" Cath asked. "Like real campers?"

Normally, the whole family was summoned to Nanny Pat's for Christmas dinner.

But this year, with her own mum's death still raw in her mind, she had decided to eat out for Christmas day – and she invited herself round to our house. Whether it was some sort of test for my mother, I couldn't be sure. But if it was, mum was anxious not to fail. She was still terrified of her mother and it was enough to rouse her out of her bed and away from her book of horror stories. I was given the job of getting the turkey cooked, but our oven was gas.

"I can't cook the turkey, we've no gas," I moaned.

"Just do it Joanne!" my mother snapped.

I went to see Mark's mum and persuaded her to let me cook it there.

"Of course," she smiled.

It had to be cooked on Christmas Eve, because she would need the oven herself on Christmas Day. Having never cooked a turkey before, I just lumped it into a tray, switched on the oven, and slammed the door.

Then, Mark and I went out to a party. I wasn't so scared of Nanny Pat any more, not since losing John. And as long as we didn't all die from food poisoning, I didn't care too much about our Christmas lunch, either.

We came home at 1am and, on the outside at least, the turkey appeared to be well roasted. I carried it home, and every now and again a globule of hot fat would drip from the end of the bag and scald my leg.

When I got home, I was met by a scene of crazy, comic chaos. Mum had plugged in a rusty Breville sandwich toaster, and she was roasting potatoes, agonisingly slowly, on the griddle.

On the kitchen work-top were pans of vegetables, and she would boil the kettle, pour it over the vegetables, and then repeat the process over and over again.

"Do you really think you can cook them by just pouring boiling water over them?" I asked incredulously.

"They'll cook eventually," my mother muttered.

I went to bed bemused, but as I lay in the dark, I could hear the kettle bubbling and my mother cursing, as she repeated the same, insane routine, all night long.

When I awoke, at 6.30am on Christmas morning, she was still blanching the vegetables. She was, in more ways than one, like a woman possessed.

I marvelled at what a motivator sheer fear could be.

We'll have packet soup as a starter," she told me. "Thank God we still have the kettle."

Nanny Pat arrived, early afternoon, with a show of festive magnanimity. She had brought presents for us all, colouring books and selection boxes.

"Where's your mother?" she asked.

"In the kitchen," I replied. "She's worked ever so hard on the dinner."

By the time it was served, mum was flushed with a combination of panic and vodka.

The potatoes were by now an encouraging rusty brown, but inside they were stubbornly hard. The vegetables, though suspiciously al dente, were edible. The turkey was slightly leathery, but it passed inspection.

I didn't eat a thing. I made my excuses and kept busy in the kitchen. But when the plates came back, they were almost empty.

Somehow, mum had pulled it off.

Still, Nanny Pat didn't over-stay the invite she had given herself, and she and Grandad made their excuses as soon as dinner was over.

It was a pity, but there was no sense of camaraderie, no self-congratulation, between mum and I. In short, no bond.

Later, Karl called round with armfuls of presents for Cath and Chris and £20 for me.

"Wow!" I whistled. "Thanks Karl."

I felt as though I had won the jackpot. I had so many plans for that money. In my head, I had already spent it a million times. But as soon as Karl left, mum pounced on me.

"Buy us some ale, Joanne," she wheedled. "Come on. It's Christmas."

Her face was white. She looked so lonely and small. I was angry with myself – and with her – but I gave her the money all the same. As I tucked the kids into bed, mum drank herself into a stupor.

The magic of Christmas proved to be just that, because early in the New Year, the water was cut off too.

"Mum!" I exploded. "Can't you just pay the bloody bill?"

She had managed to keep herself in lager all over Christmas. But not water. It was infuriating. There was a tap in our local cemetery and we sent Chris out to fill bottles. He and Cath giggled, like fugitives, as they stacked bottles behind the kitchen door. The way they carried on, it could have been rubies and emeralds they were smuggling. They loved every minute of it. But I knew I couldn't stay there. Natalie was only three weeks old and we needed running water.

"I'm going," I said flatly. "Enough is enough."

Mark's mum agreed immediately that we could stay there and I packed that same afternoon. It broke my heart to leave Cath and Chris again. They'd had so much disappointment, so many false promises, in their short lives.

"I will be back every day," I told them. "I'm not going far."

# CHAPTER 13

As good as my word, I put Natalie in the pram each morning and went back home, to check they were going to school. The house was as bad, as filthy, as squalid, as it had ever been. The windows were so dirty it was impossible to see out and they were buzzing with sticky flies. The floor was black, with a layer of grease and grime on the carpet. Somewhere, underneath a pile of bin bags and boxes, was a dining table. The kitchen was disgusting. The sink was crammed with dirty dishes, with no water to wash them. The fridge was filled with rotting food, it had never been emptied when the electricity was disconnected and now the smell was positively eye-watering.

Mum had a Yorkshire terrier called Adam and two cats, a small black one called Lucy and a big fat ginger Tom named Jacob. They had litter trays, but they were overflowing with mess, and they stank.

"Let the cats out, the house is rancid," I told her.

But mum refused.

"I'm worried they'll be knocked over on the railway line," she explained. "I like to keep them indoors."

She seemed to think more about the cats than she did about her own children. One day, I found her calmly cooking fishfingers for the cats, whilst Cath and Chris played in the street. I took in the scene and erupted.

"How come you can feed the cats and not the kids?" I yelled.

Mum had an answer ready.

"I can explain to the kids when we've no money for food," she replied. "It's different with cats. They don't understand."

I didn't know what to say. I felt she was beyond redemption. All I could do was look after Cath and Chris, the best I could.

I put my name down for a house with the council, and in April 1989 we got a letter to say we had our own place, at last. I was so excited. People were kind, donating an old dinner set or a rickety dining table, to start us off. Mark's mum gave us a lot. Nanny Edith, as ever my guardian angel, bought us a bed, a couch and chairs, and downstairs carpets. Upstairs, I nailed blankets to the floorboards to keep the place warm. I was fastidiously, clinically, clean too. I'd learned the hard way from the best teacher — mum. Nanny Edith also paid for driving lessons and had me insured on her car, a bright yellow Lada. I was allowed full use of it and borrowed it every day to nip in and check on Cath and Chris. They were only a 10-minute drive away. When there was no water or heating, I could load them into the car and bring them back to my house for a good wash and a warm-up. Somehow, mum ended up tagging along too. Despite everything, she was my mother, and it would have taken a heart of stone to leave her alone in a cold, dark house. And I knew it would have upset Cath and Chris too, to leave her out. Even so, it seemed beyond tolerant, beyond stupid, for me to cook her dinner and wash her clothes. But I did it.

One afternoon, when I was calling in, Julie's mum stopped me in the street.

"Your mum has put a lot of weight on recently," she said deliberately. "I think you should know."

I had a good idea what she was trying to tell me. She wanted to help. She wasn't a gossip.

"I've got my own shit going on," I sighed. "I can't keep looking after her."

Even so, I did notice mum was bulging under her clothes. She was definitely an odd shape. But then, I reasoned, she was an odd woman. And it was pointless asking her what was going on. I had long since given up trying to get the truth out of her.

Those times with Cath and Chris were golden. I loved cooking a Shepherd's pie or a roast chicken and seeing their faces light up with anticipation. After tea, we'd play Cluedo or Monopoly until it was time for me to take them back home to bed. I hoped that my house could be a little sanctuary for them, as Nanny Edith's had been, and still was, for me.

I worried in particular about Cath. I made sure she went to school every day, but I knew she was picked on and bullied a little, because she didn't have the coolest clothes or the trendiest trainers. Mum didn't buy her anything. Instead, we relied on hand-me-downs and presents. Julie's mum would give us bin-bags filled with secondhand clothes and Cath and I would tip them on the carpet and 'ooh' and 'aah' like we had discovered a treasure trove.

Whenever I had any money, I would buy Cath a little treat. I bought her first bra. It was me, too, she came to when her periods started.

"You're growing up," I said proudly, blinking back my emotion.

I began buying two lots of sanitary towels with my shopping. It was pointless relying on mum.

Cath was mad on the band, Take That, and for one birthday I bought her a Mark Owen doll. But she and Chris were forever arguing and in one spat, he beheaded the doll and hung it from the lampshade.

"See how Mark Owen likes that," he said with a smirk.

It was a typical boy's trick, but Cath was inconsolable. She cried for days and I had no money to buy her another.

"You've always got me," I told her. "Always."

And that was enough for us both. She could talk to me, about anything at all. I was mother, sister and best friend. And as time went on, our relationship became less of a responsibility and more of a privilege.

But with Mark, life was not so straightforward. Even with a baby to look after, he had continued to drink heavily. He had stopped working, and I found myself holding down three jobs, working in a local farm shop, cleaning for an agency, and selling Betterware products door to door. I was always on the go.

As time went on, I realised, with a sinking heart, that I had chosen a male replica of my own mother. And yet, as with her, I soldiered on and kept my problems to myself. I couldn't walk out on anyone. I couldn't make a stand. And I didn't understand why.

"You spend every penny on drink, you're just like her!" I would yell at Mark.

And he would scowl and snap open another can of lager.

"Give her a break," he'd say. "You're the problem. Not me. Not your mother."

Our rows went round in circles and we got nowhere. One afternoon, we were in the middle of a barney when two of Mark's mates called round. I strapped Natalie into the buggy, keen to get outside for some air, but I got the wheels jammed as I tried to get through the hallway and out of the house.

"Do you need a hand?" asked one of Mark's mates.

His name was Tom and he was only trying to be helpful. But I grunted and shook my head and eventually clattered outside, for a long walk with Natalie. When I got back, they had gone, and Mark had disappeared down to the pub. But afterwards, Tom came round more often. He and Mark would sit up together, until late. I was resentful of Mark, because I had to get up early for work. But Tom seemed kind and friendly. He didn't drink like Mark and he had a good job, too.

When Natalie was three years old, I fell pregnant again. With Natalie, I had loved every minute of the pregnancy, but this was different. I was very sick and, no matter what I tried, I lost lots of weight. Worried, I had extra ante-natal appointments and checks. But my midwife assured me the baby was perfectly healthy. Then, by the time I was seven months pregnant, I could barely walk with back pain.

"It's one thing after another with you," Mark grumbled, as though I was making it up.

"This is your baby as well," I reminded him sharply.

One Sunday night in September 1992, my labour began, very slowly at first. It was four days later – and my 21st birthday — before my contractions finally got into a regular rhythm and I realised it was time to pack my hospital bag. Stubbornly, I insisted on watching an episode of *Brookside* before Mark and I went off to hospital. It was my favourite programme and the least I could ask for on my landmark birthday, I reckoned. Mum, still a better grandmother than a mother, offered to look after Natalie. But I made sure Cath was there too, fussing over her and in overall charge.

Our daughter, Samantha, was born that same night at 11:25pm, weighing 6lb 13ozs. She didn't look at all like

Natalie or John – my first impression was that she was just like my dad. Holding her in my arms, her blue eyes staring intently at mine, I fell in love, all over again.

"What a birthday present!" I cooed.

Mark wasn't the most hands-on father, though he clearly loved his children. And in his defence, I was very protective, to the point of shutting him out. I didn't let anyone look after my girls. So, whilst he was out drinking, I was quite happy to be at home with our daughters. Sometimes I actually looked forward to him going out so that I could have them to myself. And besides, when we were together, we were at loggerheads. Our relationship was increasingly stormy. We had vicious rows, especially when he was drunk. It got so bad, the police came out occasionally. Yet I didn't let that upset me too much. Mark mattered less to me now than ever. I had my two little princesses – the family I had always dreamed of – and they were my whole world. I didn't need him at all.

# CHAPTER 14

When Samantha was two months old, Grandad John, my dad's dad, died. He had struggled ever since his stroke and in a way, it was a relief that he was no longer suffering. But I missed him terribly. He and Nanny Edith had been the only shining lights in such a dark childhood. And now Edith was on her own, and so I spent more and more time with her. She adored my two daughters and we loved being with her. Mark wasn't a part of it. But I was glad.

The following year, Uncle Bernard, Nanny Pat's son, died from a suspected heart attack. After the funeral, the family gathered at her house. In the posh lounge, with the embossed walls and the sickly smell, Bernard's wife began to cry, quietly.

"What are you crying for?" Nanny Pat snapped, rounding on her. "I've lost a son. I've lost a child. Why are you crying?"

There was an awkward silence. And suddenly, my blood boiled and I erupted. I saw Nanny Pat for what she was, a disgraceful bully and a venomous hypocrite. I no longer feared her or respected her.

"How dare you?" I thundered. "How dare you?"

I was shaking with white-hot anger.

"I lost a child too," I hissed. "Do you remember? My son died. You didn't want to talk about it then. So let's talk about it now."

The room emptied. I was on my own. But that was nothing new. I stood over Nanny Pat, spitting with rage. I was so angry, I was even scaring myself.

She seemed to deflate before my eyes. To my amazement, I realised she was weeping, her head in her hands, her shoulders sagging. I left her there, sobbing, and banged out of the house, feeling strangely proud of myself. After all these years, I had spoken up for my son. I had done it at last.

"Not before time," I told myself.

In the weeks afterwards, Nanny Pat was surprisingly civil and decent towards me. It was as if, by standing up to her, I had gained her respect. And from then on, we got along fine from her perspective. I still harboured a lot of resentment towards her – I always would. As a person, I didn't like her much at all. But I had had my say and now I was willing to tolerate her. Also, she had aged quickly after her son's death and she looked frail and vulnerable. Softening, I invited her over for tea occasionally. I visited her too with my daughters. I took Cath to see her. And she approved of my little family, because they were clean, tidy and well-mannered. It was not a reconciliation, but it was a slight thaw. This was as good as it was going to get. It was the best I could do.

In June 1994, Nanny Pat went away to Northumberland for a few days with her daughters, including mum, and Cath went along too. But two days into the holiday, they had to come home, because Nanny Pat was ill. Cath rang me and her voice was sombre.

"Nanny Pat is not expected to last the night," she said. "You should come and see her."

She had always had heart problems. She was a heavy smoker, and of course, losing her mother and her son had hit her badly. It was as if everything had got too much for her.

I went into the bedroom, very briefly, and looked at Nanny Pat in the bed, barely conscious.

"Right, I've seen her," I said to Cath. "I'm going now."

Downstairs, the whole family was gathered. Nanny Pat was not simply the head of the family. She was the fear of the family too. They had to be here.

"There is no way she's going into hospital," Grandad Bernard vowed. "She was always very clear about that. She spent her whole life working in a hospital, and she wants to die at home."

And so, in the end, she passed peacefully, surrounded by her surviving children. Despite her iron will, her heart had stuttered to a final stop.

Nanny Pat had always been scared of spiders, so it was decided she would be cremated, to save her that final terror of burial. I went to her funeral, but I was dry-eyed. I couldn't have cried, not for her.

I would have been a liar to say I was sad to see her go. I blamed her for many things, not least my mum's problems and my son's death. But I felt sad for the relationship we'd never had, for the bond we'd never shared. I ached for what had been missing. I grieved not for the woman she was, but for the woman I wish she had been.

# CHAPTER 15

Two deaths in the family were a reminder that life was short. My day to day life with Mark was so miserable, for us both. And, as summer 1996 approached, I began to think seriously about making a change.

I knew Mark would never agree to a separation, not without a fight. But one day, on the school run, I spotted a house for rent. It was small and neat with a nice garden for the girls. And it got me thinking.

The next day, after dropping Natalie at school, I called in at the estate agents.

"We would need £100 deposit and a month's rent upfront," smiled the agent.

My heart sank. I couldn't get my hands on that sort of money, not without Mark noticing at any rate.

"Would you like to look around?" the agent asked.

And immediately, without thinking, I nodded. She grabbed a set of keys and off we went. I didn't know what

I was doing. There was no way I could afford it. Looking round would just torture me with the promise of what might have been.

The door swung open and straightaway I got a good feel about the place. It was clean and airy and there were two neat little bedrooms for the girls.

"It's perfect," I sighed.

That night, whilst Mark slept, I racked my brains. I knew that my aunt Dish could and probably would lend me the money. But pride stood in my way. I had always been so fiercely independent. I felt like a failure, asking her for help.

The following morning, over breakfast, Mark and I had a furious row over something so trivial it was almost laughable. But it helped to make up my mind. I called Dish and told her my plan.

"Of course I'll lend you the money," she said. "I'll do what I can."

She never spoke about the way mum was. Her drinking was never mentioned. But I got the feeling she was helping me out to compensate. It was her way of addressing the problem without admitting there was a problem. Nanny Pat had taught her well.

I signed for the house and I was a bundle of nerves. Secretly, I began packing toys and some clothes, items Mark hopefully wouldn't miss.

He wasn't in a regular job, but on our moving date, as luck would have it, he had been offered a day's work with a pal.

"I'll be out all day," he told me.

It was all I could do not to cheer out loud. I felt as though the stars were aligned in our favour. The moment Mark left for work, a bunch of my mates came and began unloading furniture and clothes from the house. I tried to split everything evenly between me and Mark.

By the time he came home from work that night, we had gone. I didn't leave a forwarding address. I didn't want the hassle. The girls were too young to understand what was going on and they were thrilled with their new bedrooms and a nice new garden. Samantha was due to start school the following day and they were excited about that, too.

But late at night, as I unpacked, I suddenly realised with a groan that I had left Samantha's brand new school uniform hanging up on the lounge door back at home.

"Joa!" I cursed myself. "You idiot!"

I called Cath to come and keep and eye on the girls, and I made the short trip back to my old house. Mark's car was on the drive. I knew by now he would be seething, calling everyone we knew for information. Quietly, I crept up the drive, and I could see his shadow behind the living room blinds, as he paced the room. Sure enough, he was on the phone.

I spotted an air vent, near the ground, and I dropped down and lay full length on the concrete, with my ear to the vent. Anyone passing would think I had taken leave of my senses, and the mental image almost gave me the giggles. "You'll never make a cat burglar," I told myself sternly.

The idea worked a treat. I could hear every word.

"No idea where she is at all," he was saying. "I'm going to go the school in the morning and wait until she drops the kids off. Then I can follow her back to her new place."

Scrambling quickly to my feet, I ran off, down the path. The next morning, I called school to explain the girls wouldn't be in until lunchtime, and instead I dropped them with Cath. And then, whilst I knew Mark was waiting at the school-gates, I drove back to our old house and got Samantha's uniform, a cute little grey pinafore with a red cardigan.

Cath and I laughed about my escapade later that night.

"You could start a private detective agency," she giggled. "I'll be your right hand woman."

Those first few days were bliss but Mark inevitably discovered where we were living and he started calling round to see the girls.

"I am sorry, you know," he said to me. "I do love you."

I didn't want to hear it. Despite all my resolve, I could feel myself crumbling. He visited almost every day. Until, eventually, he stayed overnight.

"I'll be different," he promised. "We can start again. Let's give it a go."

And so, stupidly faithful and faithfully stupid, I took him back.

\*\*\*

It was New Year's Eve 1997 and Mark and I had decided to throw a small party. He loved any excuse to get blind drunk, and I liked getting everyone together – Cath and Chris and our closest friends. Mark's friend, Tom, came along and I noticed he didn't drink at all. I liked that. And of course, mum came too. I hadn't the heart to leave her out. Growing up with mum and then Mark, I had learned to lower my standards of expectation, and I was impressed by a man who didn't drink. Tom was as quiet and unassuming and effortlessly comfortable with himself, as Mark was brash and braggy and desperate to prove his masculinity.

Mum wore a blue velvet dress and she had made an effort with some make-up, though she'd put on weight again, I noticed. She had quite a bulge around her middle. But, I reasoned, her arms were quite chubby too. We all knew she was the sort to put on weight and lose it again so I didn't give it too much thought. She was only 4'11 so when she put a few pounds on, they showed dramatically. She was not the sort of woman who could hide being overweight. She drank heavily that night, cosied up to Mark, regaling him with outlandish stories.

"Probably all lies," I thought sourly. "Typical mum."

That night, fuelled maybe by bitterness, I drank more than usual myself, and I had to go to bed early, feeling sick.

The following morning, Cath and I were the only ones up early. Bleary-eyed, we cleared away ashtrays and dirty glasses. But even through my fuzziness, I could tell Cath had something playing on her mind. I could read her like a book – as a mother is with a child, which after all, was what I was to her.

"Joa – what do you make of this?" she said suddenly.

I stopped, sat down and patted the couch next to me.

"Sit down," I said gently. "What's the matter?"

"Last night, at the party, I overheard mum telling people that she was pregnant," she said. "What do you think?"

Her words sent a chill down my spine. In a way, it was no big surprise. I had no doubt that Cath was telling the truth. But I knew, from weary experience, that mum was a compulsive liar and a terminal flirt. I could picture the scene perfectly, I had seen it so many times before – mum, tipsy, desperate for attention, sidling up to men she barely knew on the couch.

"She might well have announced she was pregnant as a way of getting sympathy," I said thoughtfully to Cath. "She loves a spot of drama. You know that."

Then again, I knew she could well be telling the truth, too. After all, I had no idea how many men she had slept with. She'd had a boyfriend, a local bloke, quite recently. He'd seemed rather nice and normal, but mum had dropped him, before Christmas, with no explanation.

"He was probably too normal," I'd smirked to Cath, at the time.

Neither of us had any idea what she was thinking. It was impossible to know her, and to know what she was like, because I very much doubted she even knew what she was like herself. But I felt convinced that she was incapable of showing any affection or attention unless it was sexual. I knew too it was pointless to confront her, because she would just lie compulsively. Some lies were outlandish, ridiculous and fantastic. Other times, she would garnish her lies with snippets of truth, so that it was difficult to pick through what was and what wasn't real. I felt, more and more, that mum's grip on reality and the truth was slipping, and that she was beginning to believe her own bull-shit. She had, effectively, brainwashed herself.

"We should keep an eye on her," I said to Cath. "That's all we can do."

Cath agreed to check mum's shopping, to see if she was buying sanitary towels.

"Try and get a look at her stomach when she's getting dressed," I suggested. "You'll have to peep round the bedroom door. Look out for swollen ankles. Stretch marks. Mid-night cravings. That sort of thing."

Cath wrinkled her nose in disgust and we both laughed. It was a strange mission, doing under-cover surveillance on our own mother.

"Surely it should be the other way round," Cath complained. "Mum should be worrying about us getting pregnant."

I nodded. She was quite right. But of course, things had been the wrong way round for many years. And that wasn't about to change.

Later that week, I called in, more to check on Cath than to see mum. I was worried about her carrying such a big secret around. She was, after all, still a child. Looking around the living room, I felt a flash of anger. The place was disgusting. I hadn't intended to confront mum at all but when I saw her, propped up against the doorway, her stomach rounded, my mouth got the better of me.

"Your stories have a way of leaking out," I said irritably. "You should be careful what you say."

I looked pointedly at her stomach, trying to figure out how to word the next bit.

"You know," I nodded.

Mum sucked in her breath sharply.

"Don't be ridiculous," she snapped.

She turned and marched off upstairs and that was that.

"She won't admit it," I whispered to Cath. "But she'll have to tell us eventually. I can't see her going through with the birth all on her own. She certainly won't want to look after a baby. That's not her style."

The weeks went on. I was more and more worried about Cath. But my own life was unravelling too. Mark and I were at war. Each day seemed to bring a new argument, a different problem. He was still drinking heavily, still without a steady job, and I resented him more and more.

"We've two children to think of," I snapped. "You need to step up."

I tried to insist on him drinking once a week only – usually on a Friday night. But he rarely kept to it.

Cath knew I was having trouble with Mark and she was becoming my shoulder to cry on, more so than I was hers. I was aware my life was in a mess and I hated it. I had always been the reliable one, level-headed and trustworthy.

I didn't want my own relationship problems to stand in the way of me looking after my own children and my brother and sister.

But one night, while Cath and I were pulling Mark to pieces, she suddenly blushed and stammered: "I've met someone myself, Joa. Nothing's happened yet but I hope it will. I really like him."

I smiled, but I could hear the uncertainty in her voice.

"That's great," I said warily. "What's the catch?"

Cath sighed.

"He's quite a bit older than me," she replied. "Ten years."

Immediately, my guard was up.

"Cath," I shrieked. "No way. That's not right. I don't want you going out with someone that old. What a pervert!"

She and I had always been able to talk things through. Her first heartbreak, a boy in school, had hit her bad. Aged 14, she had locked herself in her room and sobbed. I had bought her sweets and a can of lemonade from the shop and coaxed her out of it.

"He's not worth it," I told her. "None of them are."

We'd stayed close, too, throughout her teenage tantrums. She'd been through what I had christened her 'Kevin the Teenager' phase, where she would stand at the top of the stairs and shout: "It's not fair!"

She had stayed out late a couple of times too, and I had grounded her and read her the riot act. Never once did she accuse me of interfering. She never pointed out that I was not her mum and I had no right to discipline her. Instead, she accepted the punishment but bawled "It's not fair!"

She slammed doors and played her Take That songs at full blast and I chuckled secretly. And soon enough, the hormones settled and she was back to her old self.

But from the look on Cath's face, this time, she'd got it bad. She was swooning. If nothing else, I supposed her daydreams were a distraction from the weird reality of her home-life. I could only hope the crush would pass.

# CHAPTER 16

I called in to see mum every few days, with a bag of shopping. Or I'd just stop by for a coffee and give the kitchen and bathroom a once-over with a cloth.

And her stomach grew. And grew. I didn't know what to think.

"Perhaps she's overdoing the cakes," I decided.

She'd always had a sweet tooth. It was the easiest thing to think. But funnily enough, I noticed she was drinking less, too. I felt uneasy.

"You need to get on the exercise bike," I joked, nodding at her bump. "You're piling on the pounds."

I knew it was useless to confront her directly again.

In March 1998, mum announced she was doing a 'house-swap'.

"I'm swapping with one of the neighbours," she told me. "I've always hated this house. I can't wait to move."

She was only moving around the corner. But her house was in such a state and I knew it would be a big job to tidy up all the mess.

"Do you want me to help you move?" I asked. "I don't mind."

I did mind. I minded an awful lot. And even as I spoke, I wondered why on earth I was putting myself out for her – yet again. It was a question I couldn't really answer. For me, looking after my mum was a way of life. Ever since I was a little girl, I had covered for her and cleaned up after her – it was automatic to me. I had brought up her two children for goodness sake – and myself too. A part of me pitied her. I went from savaging to salvaging her character, sometimes in the same single thought process. As I got stronger, mum was becoming weaker, more fragile. She needed me, because she had nobody else. Besides, I couldn't possibly have enlisted any outside help, the shame would have been too much for me to bear. I wanted to keep mum's dirty secrets, and her dirty house, to myself.

But at first, mum refused to let me near the packing. She wouldn't even let me upstairs to size up the task.

"I'll manage," she snapped.

But as the weeks went by, and the date drew nearer, she was forced to relent. She had nobody else but me.

"Will you help me?" I asked Mark. "It'll be a big job."

The following weekend, I hired a transit van, bought a pack of rubber gloves, and braced myself. But as mum opened the door, and we stepped inside, Mark suddenly clamped his hand over his mouth and backed away.

"I can't go in there," he said in a muffled voice. "It's horrendous. The smell is disgusting."

I stared, open-mouthed, as he disappeared off up the street, leaving me to manage on my own.

I was expecting a mess. But I got so much worse. In every corner, there was pile after pile of rubbish. There was cat and dog shit in the kitchen, even though she hadn't kept dogs for years. I actually found a dirty nappy – partly rotted and matted into the carpet – from thirteen or fourteen years earlier.

Pinned to one of the many bin bags was a handwritten note, on a scrap of paper, which said: 'Nobody should live like this.'

I presumed it was from one of mum's recent boyfriends, who had decided to vent his disgust before walking out on her.

"She probably never read it," I said under my breath as I scrunched it up. "Waste of ink. Waste of paper."

I opened the washing machine door and retched at the stench of rotting clothes. It had been broken for years now, yet the wet washing had never been emptied. The clothes were all stuck together, long since dried out, but mouldy and decomposing.

"For God's sake, mum," I grumbled.

It was impossible to see the colour of any carpets or curtains. I struggled even to find the back door – it was hidden behind a huge midden of bin bags.

"Why me?" I wept inwardly. "Why?"

For hours, I filled black bin bags of rubbish, ready for the refuse tip. It took me the whole weekend to empty the house.

"It would have been easier to bring the tip here," I said drily.

But mum didn't seem to see the joke. She made no apology, in fact no comment at all, about the sorry state of her environment.

"Could you not have tidied up?" I demanded. "Maybe just once in a while?"

"Couldn't be arsed," she drawled.

And that summed her up, really.

In every room, there were mounds of crap, upon crap, upon crap.

It's sad, but when I had finished, there was very little left to take to the new house. Most of what she owned was, quite literally, rubbish.

Later on, as mum unpacked a box of books inside her new living room, I noticed, from the side, that she was really gaining weight again.

Mum caught my gaze and gave a half-smile.

"I know, I know, I'm eating too much chocolate," she admitted.

And that was that.

That May, Natalie made her first communion. It was a big family occasion. I went from one shop to the next until Natalie, now nine, found the dress of her dreams. It cost me a week's wages but it was worth it to see the smile on her little face.

I bought myself a new outfit. Nanny Edith and mum both came along. And even mum had made an effort, in a black dress. But as she walked into the church, my breath caught in my throat.

Mum had a very definite bump. A baby bump.

I stared, transfixed. Was she? Wasn't she? She absolutely was. I spotted Nanny Edith staring at her, too.

But all too soon the priest was welcoming the congregation, and I looked at Natalie through misty eyes and forgot, or tried hard to forget, all about mum and her mystery bump.

A few days later, mum called and asked if Cath could come and stay with me.

"I have a bad chest," she told me. "I was wondering if you could look after Cath? I'm not up to it."

Immediately, I knew this was it. The baby. But as was the family way, we said nothing. It was what we didn't say – what we didn't do – that was most dangerous. I collected Cath and mum didn't even come outside to say hello.

"I'm so glad to get out of there," Cath breathed with a sigh of relief. "There's something up with mum."

I loved having her to stay. It was a comfort just to know she'd had a bath and a hot meal every night. And she had GCSE exams coming up at school, I tried persuading her to work hard and knuckle down. But she had missed so much school over the years, that it was too late to start catching up now. Instead, Cath was off out with her mates most of the time, having fun, shopping, hanging round the local park. I didn't mind that either, because at least she was enjoying being a teenager. It was a luxury I'd never had and I wanted it for her.

"Home by 9pm," I told her. "And not a minute later."

I was still more mother than big sister to her. And by the way her eyes smiled when she pulled a cross face, she was happy that I was.

One week later, mum rang again. I was hoping and dreading that she would announce the birth of our half-sister or brother. But I was way off the mark.

"I'm much better now," she said cheerfully. "Send Cath home."

I felt sick inside. Where was the baby? I hung up, knowing I was being lied to.

"Maybe she gave birth and then had it adopted?" Cath suggested.

"Not in just a week," I said. "She couldn't get rid of a baby that fast."

I was starting to think we were all going mad. Poor Cath didn't want to go home, but we had no option. I was no longer scared of mum. But Cath was. And she was too compliant to defy her.

"I'm only two minutes away," I promised her as I dropped her off. "I can be there at the drop of a hat. Just call me."

I felt rotten as she disappeared from view into the house. Driving home, I couldn't help feeling I had let her down.

Then, just an hour later, the phone rang, and it was Cath, agitated, tripping over her words.

"The house stinks, Joa," she babbled. "Mum told me she burned some bacon. It had gone past the sell-by date but she cooked it anyway and it smelled. But that's not it. She's lying. Something evil has happened. I know it has.

"God the smell, Joa. Honestly, it's putrid, really bad."

My blood was icy cold but I reminded myself, soundlessly, that I was the adult and I had to calm Cath down.

"I don't want you looking for −anything," I said firmly. "Let me do it. Just stay in your room. I'll be over as soon as Mark gets home to look after the girls.

"If mum goes out, call me."

I felt queasy. Still, a part of me clung to the possibility that this might not be happening. It was mad, macabre and totally and hilariously deranged. Surely there was a reasonable explanation instead.

"Maybe it *is* burned bacon after all," I muttered to myself. "She's just a yo-yo dieter who cremated her dinner."

I switched on a DVD for the kids and we settled down on the couch. But the phone rang again. This time, I heard Cath's strangled scream before the phone even reached my ear.

"What?" I demanded. "What the hell has happened?"

She was yelling hysterically, uncontrollably. In the background I could hear the sound of traffic whizzing past the phone box, almost drowned out by her wailing. It seemed darkly comic for people to be calmly driving by whilst she was making such a racket.

"Cath," I said, as evenly as I could. "Calm down. Take a breath."

"I found it!" she gulped. "Oh God, I've found it. I felt the head."

Revulsion bubbled up my throat, so acrid I almost had to spit it out.

"Go on," I said, gentle and calm in my panic. "Tell me, slowly."

"It's in a red bin, inside the wardrobe," she sobbed. "I felt the head, through a bin liner."

"Oh Christ," I croaked. "I'm on my way."

I hung up and left the house, still in my slippers, bundling the girls into their car seats.

"We're going on a little ride to find Aunty Cath," I chirped, in a voice so tinny and false I actually thought I might frighten them.

But they adored Cath, and they chanted her name all the way there.

When we arrived, Cath was waiting at the front of the house, retching into long-dead flowerbeds. There was no sign of mum. As soon as she spotted me, she scrambled into the car and screamed:

"Drive! Just drive!"

I had never in my life seen anyone so terrified, so haunted. It tore at my heart.

"Cath's not well," I told the girls.

When we got back, mercifully, Mark was home. I took the girls inside and then went back to the car. Cath had her knees hunched right up to her chest. She seemed almost catatonic with shock.

"Don't worry, I'll sort this out," I reassured her, patting her knee.

But in truth, my head was spinning. I had no idea what to do. Did I call the police – or a doctor – or a priest? Part of me still doubted that it was happening at all. It was the stuff of horror films, the stuff mum loved reading in her monthly magazines. She'd been catapulted from a mere fan to the star of the show.

"Bingo, mum," I said through clenched teeth.

Cath sat in the passenger seat and sobbed.

"Mum went out to the garage for fags," she wept. "I decided to have a look in her bedroom. In the wardrobe, I found a red bin – like Dusty Bin off the telly, you know... there were insects crawling all over the lid. And the smell. Oh god."

She shuddered and retched a little. I squeezed her hand.

"You're doing well," I whispered. "Carry on."

"I lifted the lid and I reached inside," she said. "And then I felt it. Through the bin liner.

"A head. A baby's head Joa. For definite."

It was stomach-churning, every word of it. As grotesque and obscene as it was gloriously gripping.

"Did you put the lid back on?" I asked suddenly.

Cath nodded numbly.

"I'm not daft," she replied, with a shade of her usual self. "I left it just as I found it. I told mum I was coming to stay with you for the weekend and she didn't really seem to care. I don't think she's very well."

"I bet she's not," I said bitterly.

Cath was in such a state. I couldn't take her in the house, not with Mark and the girls. Instead, I took her to the pub, at the top of the road, and I bought us both a large brandy.

"Medicinal," I said. "We've had a bit of a shock."

"You can say that again," huffed Cath.

And for some reason, we both fell about laughing until the tears streamed down our cheeks. Even when I wanted to stop, I couldn't. I became frightened that I was losing control, that I wouldn't ever stop laughing, and I'd be carried out of the pub and straight off to the mental institute where Nanny Pat's ghost probably prowled the corridors. My sides ached, my head hurt, and yet still I laughed, a mad, sad, monstrous, laugh. People in the pub stared and ogled us.

# CHAPTER 17

Cath stayed with me for the whole weekend. Whenever Mark was out of earshot we talked about the baby. I asked her constantly about what had happened.

"Tell me again about the red bin," I asked her. "Every detail."

Part of me couldn't actually believe it still. I needed to hear it again and again, to make it seem real. More than anything, I was worried about Cath and her own state of mind. I felt sure that talking about it would do her good. I was determined to break the family cycle of letting secrets fester behind the net curtains.

On the second night, I dreamed of John, my own baby, and the feel of his warm, round, head against my chest, as we shared those few precious moments of love together. But then there were maggots crawling over my hands, dripping from the light switches, oozing out of the hospital bed. And I woke in a cold sweat, gasping for breath, shouting his name.

"I have to talk to mum," I said to Cath, the next morning. "We can't leave the baby there. It's not right."

I was still undecided what to do, who we should tell. Desperate for support, I spoke to Mark.

"Mum's got a dead baby in the wardrobe," I told him.

He raised his eyebrows.

"Nah!" he replied. "I think you're getting carried away with yourself there, Joanne."

He sounded almost scathing, and I knew I was wasting my time. I wasn't surprised by his reaction. Like a lot of men, he was easily taken in by mum. She was good at manipulating the opposite sex – with sex. It was a sort of reverse, perverse type of grooming, I suppose. I was going to get no help from him. I was on my own. As usual.

"Let me come with you," Cath pleaded. "Don't go by yourself."

But I was adamant. I wanted to shield her from this. She had already been through too much. By Sunday evening, I could bear it no longer. I knew this and I could not, could never, unknow it. It was spreading and ulcerating, with a cancerous stranglehold on my consciousness.

Knowing mum would not say no to a drink, I called round and offered to take her to The Coach and Horses, the pub opposite her house. My nerves jangled as I stood at the bar, ordering drinks. I was clumsy, dropping my money on the floor, my hands sweaty and cold. Anyone else would have noticed what a state I was in. But not my mum. Or if she did, she didn't care enough to ask me what was wrong.

"I'll have another vodka," she said, as she drained her glass.

It was a statement, not a request, and I traipsed back to the bar. After two vodkas, I took her home. Even now, I was hoping for a rational explanation, a pop-up way out, at the last minute. Once we were in the hallway I drew in a big breath.

"What happened to your baby?" I asked.

Mum rounded and there was a dangerous glint in her eye.

"I don't know what you're talking about," she spat. "Don't be silly."

I had expected this. But it was still hard.

"Cath found the baby in the red bin," I persisted. "We know all about it. You need help. You need a doctor."

A flicker of recognition, resignation, perhaps, passed across her face. "It's upstairs," she said. "It was born dead."

There was a moment of silence. I had expected to feel anger. Revulsion. Repugnance. Instead, I was filled with an overwhelming sense of sadness. I felt suddenly exhausted, tearful and afraid. This was confirmation. The baby, my little brother or sister, had existed. Upstairs, in the red bin, was a human being with a tiny heart and soul no bigger than a rosebud. Life snuffed out so cruelly before it had even begun.

"What do you plan to do now?" I asked.

Mum shrugged, as though she really hadn't thought this far ahead.

I closed my eyes and thought of my own lost John. The way his tiny little fingers had curled around mine. For 30 minutes, he had breathed. They were 30 glorious minutes of possibility, of hope, of happiness. And after he took his final breath, I knew, even at the age of 15, that I would never feel true happiness again. I couldn't let this baby die without so much as a goodbye.

"We have to bury the baby," I insisted. "You have to give it some dignity and respect."

To my surprise, she didn't object. And so, I pressed on.

"You need to get some help," I said.

But now, she rankled.

"I'm fine, I'm absolutely fine," she replied.

She waved me away like I was trying to give her painkillers for a headache.

"Let me talk to Dish," I suggested. "She could help."

Mum's sister, Dish, was a social worker. But mum butted in before I'd even finished my sentence. She wouldn't entertain the idea.

"Don't tell anyone," she said harshly.

The baby needs to be buried," I choked. "You can't leave it to rot in a bin. You have to do the decent thing."

Mum shrugged again, this time impatiently, as though I was trying to talk her into a night-out she didn't much fancy.

"If you want to bury it, you do it," she sighed. "It's nothing to do with me."

It's everything to do with you, I thought fiercely. And that's the problem.

I leaned against the hallway wall and gulped in some air. I was reeling. We couldn't inform the authorities and have a proper funeral. I couldn't go to the police or even a doctor. Mum would get into all sorts of trouble. She had concealed a pregnancy and a birth. She had dumped her own child in a bin. What if it hadn't been stillborn? What if? I shuddered. Despite what she was, or what she wasn't, I didn't want her to go to prison. I had to think of Cath and Chris, too. She was their mother. A poor excuse for one, but their mother nonetheless. No, we would have to bury the baby ourselves. It seemed the only option.

"We could bury it with Nanna Winnie," I suggested.

Her grave was in a large cemetery in the town centre. My little John had been buried in the same grave. And Bernard, mum's brother, had more recently been buried in there, too. I grasped onto the idea, like a lifeline..

"It's a family grave," I urged. "Nanna Winnie will look after the baby. She will understand, mum."

Mum nodded begrudgingly. Sensing that she was softening a little, I asked, "Was it a boy or a girl?"

"Girl."

"Did you give her a name?" I whispered.

Mum hesitated, unsure whether to let me in. And then, she said, "Helen."

The word pulled at my heart. She had given birth, all alone, to a stillborn child. And she had named her. I remembered my own distress, my unbearable sense of pain and emptiness, when John had died.

"Let me help you," I said tenderly.

In the future, I would look back and wonder whether mum had, at that point, manipulated me, just as she had Mark and Karl and all the other men she had picked up and dropped again. Had she really chosen a name for the baby? Or did she just want me to feel sorry for her? She was such an accomplished liar that it was hard to know. I doubted that even she knew when she was lying to herself. But in that moment, I was awash with pity and maternal care. All I could think of was baby Helen.

I knew and understood better than most the pain of losing a tiny baby so early on. "Shall we take a photo of her?" I suggested. "A memory for you? Shall we buy her some clothes?"

Mum shook her head sharply. I had gone too far now. She clammed up. Anything further had to come from me.

"I'll be back tomorrow," I told her.

And I left without another word. As I drove home, it dawned on me – that was the probably the longest conversation we'd ever had.

# CHAPTER 18

The following day, Mark needed his car for work and my own car was off the road after a bump.

"I need a car," I told him urgently. "I've got to take mum to an appointment. Can you help me out?"

I nagged until he phoned round a few friends and his mate, Tom, offered the use of his. I was so grateful.

"It's really kind of you," I smiled as he handed me the keys. "Thank you."

We decided that Cath would stay at my house, to look after my daughters. And I would take Tom's car to bury the baby.

"Be careful," Cath said to me. "What if you get into trouble?"

I shook my head and smiled. I didn't want her to worry – "I'll be fine." I said. "The baby needs a burial. I'm doing the right thing."

But inside, the dread and fear was paralysing.

On the journey, I felt cold and sick, prickling with foreboding, but resolute all the same. This had to be done.

She met me, at the door, carrying a white canvas shopping bag and I was taken aback. She looked as if we could have been off out on a hunt for bargains, maybe to a car-boot sale or a morning market.

Instead, we were off to illegally bury a dead baby.

"Oh!" I stuttered. "You're ready, then. Shall I take the bag?"

As I lifted it into the boot, it dripped with globules of blood and accusation.

My mind flashed back to that Christmas Eve, when I'd cooked the turkey for mum, in Mark's mum's oven because our gas had been disconnected at home and all the way home, the thick sticky blobs of fat from the turkey had dripped from the bag and splashed onto my legs, scalding and stinging.

I'd got her out of a mess back then. And I was doing it again now. But there was a big difference between globules of turkey fat and globules of baby.

We didn't speak again. Mum, because she seemed distracted, gazing out of the window, as though really she had nothing of interest to say. Me, because I was gagging so hard on the smell that it was all I could do not to vomit down my new jeans and summer top.

Parking at the cemetery, and walking through the groups of families, clustered on the paths, I was frozen stiff with fear.

It was only when we got to the grave, and I lay little Helen in the ground, that I spoke again.

"Would you like to say a few words?" I asked her.

Mum shook her head, impatiently. It was as if she had somewhere better to be. We walked back through the cemetery, side by side, but planets apart. I dropped her off at home and she left the car without a word.

Not even: "Thanks for the lift. Thanks for burying my baby. Sorry about the mess."

It was probably quite something that we had managed to get through the whole terrible ordeal, with less than a dozen words between us.

But what did I expect?

All through my childhood, I'd never really had a conversation with my mum. We exchanged information. But we didn't communicate. She heard me alright. But she never listened.

Nanny Edith listened. She really listened. And she was deaf.

When I got back home, Cath was waiting, frantic, desperate, at the window. I gave her a quick wave but went straight upstairs to strip off all my clothes, the bloody beige jeans, the flowery vest top, even the sandals – right down to my bra and knickers.

Cath's face appeared at the bedroom door.

"Fancy a bonfire?" I asked, with a grim smile. "These clothes stink. I'm going to burn the lot."

Poor Cath looked distraught.

"Are you OK?" she asked. "Did anyone see you?"

I shook my head.

Don't think so," I muttered.

"Maybe you got away with it," she said her face brightening a little.

I grimaced.

"Don't say that, Cath, don't say it. You make it sound like I was doing something wrong."

We looked at each other and we both knew, without words, that of course it was wrong. It was so bloody wrong. At that moment, I couldn't think of anything worse.

"Cath, if this ever comes out, you must promise me absolutely and completely, that you will swear you knew nothing about it," I said fiercely. "I don't want you to get into trouble. Just leave it to me."

I grabbed a box of matches and we went into the garden. Seeing my clothes take light and burn felt like such a relief.

"Not burning the evidence, just getting rid of the stench," I explained, more to myself than Cath.

But I sounded far from convinced.

"Those jeans were nearly new," Cath said faintly. "What a waste."

I shrugged.

"Stains on my jeans, stains on my soul," said a voice somewhere inside my head.

"Let's clean the car next," I said out loud. "I can't give it back to Tom like this."

I didn't tell Cath about the large clots of blood which had dripped from the bag and congealed in the car boot. But, as we snapped on our rubber gloves, I knew they would infect my nightmares and my day dreams for as long as I lived. Cath stood on the pavement, looking on in alarm, as I carried bottles of cleaner and bleach and polish outside.

"Bloody hell, Joa," she gasped. "Is it that bad?"

I scowled. It was worse. But I didn't tell her that. I opened the car door and braced myself as the fetid miasma of rotting flesh stung my eyes and nose.

"Can you smell it Cath?" I gagged.

She nodded.

"Definitely smells a bit off," she muttered in what seemed to me to be an understatement of monumental proportion.

We set about scrubbing the car. Cleaning, rubbing, polishing, spraying. My arm felt like it was going to drop off. But the pain was good. I liked it. The more I scrubbed, the better I felt.

"Joa," Cath said nervously. "I have to tell you something."

I stood back for a breather.

"A few nights before I found Helen, I woke up in the night and I heard what sounded like a baby crying," she said.

"At the time, I thought it was a cat, and I just went back to sleep. You know how cats can sound like babies when they wail.

"But now, I don't know... I just don't know." Tormented tears streamed down her cheeks.

"I keep dreaming about it," she sobbed. "Did I hear Helen crying and go back to sleep? Could I have saved her?"

"Mum said the baby was stillborn," I reminded her. "We'll never know the truth. But it was probably a cat. You're right, they sound so similar. You can't torture yourself with this Cath." I said, desperately trying to make her feel better. "We have to take mum's word for it."

Neither of us were convinced. When would we ever take mum's word for anything? But what else could I say? I grabbed my dishcloth, sprayed it with soap, and began scrubbing once again. Cath's body heaved with sobs, but she did the same. My arms burned with exhaustion.

"Can you still smell it?" I asked Cath. "Can you?"

"I don't think so," she wavered. "Well, I'm not sure."

"Right," I said. "More hot water. More soap. Let's start again."

Cath groaned. But I was on a mission. Cleaning the car felt like some sort of penance. And with good penance came the certainty of absolution. I'd managed to pick that much up at least at Sunday mass with Nanny Pat. By the time we'd finished, the car was sparkling and gleaming, cleaner than it had been brand new.

"It smells fine," Cath insisted. "Bit bleachy but fine. Honestly, Joa."

I flung the rubber gloves in the outside bin and marched upstairs, to switch the shower onto the hottest setting I could stand. Standing under the scalding water was another form of punishment and the catharsis was explosive. I washed my hair over and over. I scrubbed my arms and legs with a green brillo pad until they were raw and sore. I cut my fingernails and toenails so short that they stung. But still even under the running water, I could smell it. It felt like the stench was clinging to the inside of my nose, the underside of my eye-lids and the soles of my feet. Would I ever get rid of it?

"Go," I said fiercely, tipping another handful of shampoo onto my head. "Leave me alone."

That evening, when I took the car back to Tom, he peered inside and smiled in surprise.

"Thanks for cleaning the car," he said. "It smells great. There was no need, really."

"I spilled some milk," I mumbled. "Sorry, I've managed to clean it all up."

Back at home, I sat Cath down and reminded her again of her vow of secrecy.

"Who on earth would believe me anyway?" she said with a hard laugh. "Who could I tell? Can you imagine anyone taking me seriously?"

She did, I realised, have a point.

# CHAPTER 19

That night, I slept really, weirdly, well. I was exhausted – and knowing that baby Helen was at peace, knowing she had been buried with dignity and love, was such a comfort. I slept sound in the knowledge that I had done the wrong thing, but for the right reasons.

Then the next morning, the demon smell was there again, at the back of my throat, stinging my eyes and my nostrils, clinging to me like a nagging ghost. I just couldn't get rid of it. And I wondered if I ever would.

Thankfully my own car was ready for driving again that same week, so I didn't need Tom's car again. But one month on, Mark announced that he was going to Alton Towers for the day with Tom.

"Why don't you come?" he suggested. "Let's have some fun."

Fun was a word I hadn't heard in a long time and I decided to go. By the time the day came around, I was looking forward to it. But as Tom pulled up outside, in his car, a shiver ran through me. Mark and I clambered into the back and I suddenly gagged. The smell was back. Or perhaps it had never left.

"What's the matter?" asked Mark. "You look green."

I hesitated. I didn't understand why he couldn't smell it. But I didn't know how to broach it. I couldn't exactly say: "What's that smell?" when I knew full well what the bloody smell was. I was the only one with the answers.

To me, it was so strong, I could taste it, I could feel it stinging the mucous membrane of my nose. And yet nobody else even seemed to be aware of it. I wondered whether I was going mad, Lady-Macbeth style. I'd be seeing spots of blood next. But this was not in my imagination. There *was* a definite smell. I was sure of it.

"Open the window, Mark," I gasped. "I need some air."

He looked at me in amazement. I had a reputation for always being cold. I would usually complain like mad if anyone switched off the heating or opened a window.

All the way to Alton Towers, I felt hot and queasy. The day dragged. I sat on the grass and waited whilst Mark and Tom whizzed past on rollercoasters, screaming. All I could think of was the journey home.

"I don't know what got into you today," Mark griped, as Tom dropped us off. "You were a right misery."

I went straight upstairs for a shower. I put all my clothes on a hot wash. And I wondered whether I would ever be free from the smell.

# CHAPTER 20

The months went by and, gradually, I managed to push the memory of the burial into the back of my mind. But every time someone said the name "Helen", I would think of her, and with such sadness. When I saw baby girls in prams, maybe at the supermarket or in the street, I'd flash back to the bag and the burial.

"Helen," I murmured. "I haven't forgotten you."

As far as I knew, only three people knew of her existence. One was a child. One was emotionally AWOL. And that just left me. And so I felt a duty to remember her. I owed her that. She was my sister, after all.

Once, I bought a leg of pork for Sunday lunch, and invited Cath round. But when I got it out of the fridge, and cut the plastic wrapper, my eyes suddenly watered and I heaved.

"Oh it's that smell, I recognise it," Cath flinched. "That pork is on the turn."

I threw it away in the outside bin and washed my hands more than a dozen times. She and I hardly ate anything at our make-shift meal later but nobody, except us two, knew why. We exchanged knowing glances and I knew that she, like me, could think of nothing else but our baby sister, a bonfire in the back garden and a car that we had cleaned until our hands bled. Cath and I had a bond like no other – love and friendship, secrecy and guilt.

# CHAPTER 21

Despite the problems between Mark and I, we kept up with family traditions and routines as best we could. It was so important to me that the girls had a settled home life, big birthday and Christmas celebrations, warm meals each evening, clean clothes, fresh sheets and — above all — cuddles and love.

On New Year's Eve 1999, we threw a bit of a party. It was just a few family and close friends and, as usual, Mark was blind drunk and I grew frustrated and bored. I fancied off-loading my moans onto Cath, but I couldn't find her anywhere.

"Where's Cath?" I asked mum.

Mum shrugged, knocking back her drink.

"She mentioned something about nipping home," she slurred.

I waited a while but she didn't reappear and so I went to look for her. She had just moved into her own flat, up the road from me, so it didn't take me long. I was glad of the fresh air anyway. But when I arrived, I spotted a strange car parked outside, and I faltered.

"Surely not, Cath," I whistled, under my breath.

I knew she had a dodgy latch on her front door, and if you shoved it hard enough, you could force it open. And so I did just that. And there she was, caught in the act with a man who looked at least my age.

I felt my blood boiling. Completely ignoring Cath's mortified screams, I marched over and punched him, full in the face.

"Leave my sister alone!" I yelled.

He staggered back, stunned. And then, I marched out. I was furious. Cath was just 16 years old. How dare he? She had a lot to learn. And this was a harsh lesson.

Back at home, I left Mark drinking downstairs and I went to bed, to lie awake and curse all through the small hours. Cath was round the next morning, shame-faced. But I could see she was half-hoping I might have calmed down, and she was looking for some sort of approval from me.

"Stay away from him," I told her. "It's for your own good. He's far too old for you. You can do so much better."

But it seemed my heavy-handedness had backfired on me. Because that same week, she announced they were moving in together.

"We're serious," she told me sincerely.

"Serious my arse," I snapped.

I was still so angry. They moved into her flat and I swallowed back my bile enough to wish them both the best. But after just one night, Cath was at my door again, in tears.

"We had one night together," she sobbed. "That was all.

"He's gone. He said it wasn't working out. He's gone back to the woman he was living with."

I hated to see her so upset. But first and foremost, I was her mother figure. Her role model. And she needed tough love.

"You'll get over it," I said briskly. "You'll find someone your own age. I promise you."

And in time, that was just what she did. She settled down and grew up into such a wonderful young woman and I couldn't have been prouder of her. When she turned 18, we had a night out together in the local pubs. There was nobody I got on better with. And yet, I couldn't relax with Cath, because I still felt I had to look after her and keep a check on her.

"I don't want you drinking too much," I told her. "Take it easy."

But she laughed and replied: "You don't need to keep on mothering me, Joa. I'm a grown-up now."

I noticed, however, that she kept on disappearing outside every so often and when she returned, she smelled strongly of cigarettes.

"You've been smoking," I said accusingly. "I had no idea!"

But Cath blushed and shook her head.

"No," she stuttered. "Not really. Well, I just didn't want you to know, Joa. I didn't want to let you down. I thought you might be cross."

I was a smoker myself but she was right, I was cross. In spite of myself, I smiled. I wasn't done mothering her yet. And that was no bad thing.

There were more nights out. We went to Blackpool in fancy dress, on a hen night. Another time, we went in a limousine, for a birthday party. But I always had my eye on her. And that would never change.

Towards the end of 2000, she called in to see me and I sensed, intuitively, that she was pregnant. It was hard to put my finger on, there was something about her, her expression maybe. It wasn't necessarily physical. I just knew.

"You're having a baby," I said immediately.

Cath's jaw dropped, she was aghast.

"I've not even had it confirmed yet," she gasped. "How the hell did you know?"

I shrugged and smiled.

"Save your money on the pregnancy test," I replied. "I just know."

Her relationship with the baby's dad didn't work out. So I went along, with her to all the ante-natal checks. When the 20 week scan showed she was carrying a boy, we both whooped for joy.

Towards the end of the pregnancy, she developed a craving for ice. Every day she would call round, pull a chair into the kitchen, and sit in front of my fridge freezer, scraping off delicious slivers of frozen water.

"Can't get enough of it, Joa," she laughed.

With her due date approaching, I began teasing her about her pain threshold. She had always been such a softie and I made the most of hamming up the labour to scare her.

"It's dreadful," I told her. "You'll be in agony."

By the time her first contractions began, in April 2001, poor Cath was terrified. But she was so much braver than I gave her credit for. I was her birthing partner, and mum was there too. It was incredible, to be at the business end, to actually see a baby born. I felt anxious for Cath, and so protective, but privileged and lucky, too. With all these emotions swimming around my head, I even felt myself softening towards mum, who was sitting at the other end of the labour room, looking slightly vacant.

Even at this late stage, a small fragment of me still hoped that such a mind-blowing experience might be the trigger for some kind of bond between mum and me. But I was foolish and stupid to hope.

After baby Johnny was born, mum held him for the obligatory photo and then passed him back to Cath immediately, without even speaking.

"It's as though she's allergic to babies," I said to Cath afterwards. "Or maybe she's scared of the emotion. Maybe she just can't let herself go."

It was a puzzle. And one I was likely never to solve.

When little Johnny was three months old, Nanny Edith's neighbour called me, to say her milk was still on the doorstep, and she was concerned.

"It's just not like Edith to leave her milk out all day," she said.

I jumped in the car and drove straight round there, with a sinking feeling. I had spare keys and I let myself in, my mouth dry. I was dreading what I would find. Poor Nanny was on the kitchen floor, obviously in a great deal of pain. With difficulty, using slow, painful, sign language, she managed to tell me she had been cooking her dinner the previous evening but had slipped and fallen as she lifted a pan of potatoes off the stove.

She had been lying on the wet floor, surrounded by potatoes, for hours.

"Oh, Nan," I said tearfully.

Whilst we waited for the ambulance, I put a pillow under her head and signed words of comfort. In hospital, a scan showed that her pelvis was badly broken and her doctors warned it would be too much, given her age and her frailty, for her to recover.

"You don't know my Nanny," I said fiercely.

But I knew I was putting off the pain. Unable to face the unfaceable. For two weeks, she hung on. Cath and I took it in turns to sit with her, so that she was never alone. But on July 25 2001, aged 73, Nanny Edith's organs began to shut down, and I knew this was it. There was so much I wanted to tell her, but I was so scared of breaking down.

Instead, I rubbed her hands and stroked her face. Her skin was like parchment, and each line had once been a smile. To keep away the tears, I turned her bedside fan to blow directly in my face, and I sucked hard on polo mints. More than anything, I wanted simply to thank her. She had been my light. My kindness. My love. And when she took her last breath, I felt a tectonic shift beneath me. It was like the earth had stopped turning.

"Thank you," I whispered, softly.

In accordance with her wishes, Nanny Edith was cremated and her ashes were scattered in a memorial garden. She had left express instructions that she didn't want a headstone or a marker for her remains, because she didn't want me to upset myself by visiting.

I thought back to John's death, and Nanny Edith's kind donation for his headstone. I had never told her the truth about the headstone. But, looking back, she had understood my trauma completely. Even at the last, she had put me first.

I had her photo by my bedside and I kissed her every morning and evening. I wore her wedding and engagement rings, too. In years to come, I would lend them to my daughters, for luck on special occasions. Natalie would, in the future, wear them for her driving test. Samantha would borrow them for her finals at university. But I felt lost without them and I was always anxious to get them back.

The days without Nanny Edith were very tough. I missed her desperately. It was in the total silence of the memorial garden where I felt closest to her, the stillness and the peace there mirroring the oasis of calm in her own home. I could close my eyes and imagine her signing to me, each letter, each syllable, a silent fanfare of love. I had the girls to help keep me going, and I was grateful. But I thought of Nanny Edith each and every day, and I imagine and hope that it will be that way for the rest of my life.

Life went on, and in November 2002, I planned a surprise 21$^{st}$ birthday party for Cath, at our local social club. We invited a whole bunch of family and friends and, though the plot had leaked out to Cath, she managed to feign shock as she walked into the darkened party hall and everyone started singing.

We had a great night. But mum, true to form, was swaying drunkenly and I watched, hawk-eyed, as she sidled up to different men, flirting hopelessly, regardless of whether they were single or not. It was though she couldn't help herself, just as she couldn't bear to hold a baby, she couldn't pass up the chance to seduce passing strangers.

Tonight was about Cath. Not mum. I knocked back a stiff vodka and sighed. I was sick and tired of trying to work her out.

Early in 2003, Cath popped in to see me and, again, I felt that same sixth sense I'd had two years previously.

"You're pregnant again!" I beamed.

"Joa!" she grumbled, laughing in spite of herself. "How on earth do you do it?"

By now, she was settled with a new partner, John. There was a buzz of excitement in the family at the news of her pregnancy. I heard too, that one of our cousins, Ellie, was pregnant at the same time. The following March, Cath gave birth to a son, Connor. He was beautiful and I was so pleased for her. She was a devoted mum, caring and kind. Thankfully with Cath, as with me, the maternal pendulum had swung totally the other way, and the scars from our awful childhood had only served to make us into better, gentler, more loving parents ourselves. If anything, Cath and I spoiled our kids. They wanted for nothing. And I wouldn't have had it any other way.

But, as I cradled baby Connor, his eyes staring, wide with wonder, I had a flashback to the dripping bag, the clotted blood and the clumps of afterbirth. And the smell. Oh the smell. I swallowed but the taste was there....

"He's gorgeous Cath," I stuttered. "You've done so well."

And as I handed him back to her, I had a vision of myself, gently lowering baby Helen into the grave. I could feel the rawness on my scratched hands, the hot sun burning the back of my neck.

"What's the matter?" Cath asked in concern.

"Nothing," I beamed. "Nothing at all."

She said nothing more, but I knew she knew. I hated myself for the web of lies I had created. How could this have happened? How could I be in this situation, after what happened to John?

I had been so scathing of the gauze of secrecy which shrouded Nanny Pat's life. I had derided her for her guiding principles of hypocrisy and dishonesty. Yet now, I was just the same. And I had despised my mother too, for her drinking and her fecklessness. Yet in Mark, I had found her male equivalent. I had tried so hard, too hard, to escape the monstrous women of my past and I'd actually ended up an imperfect hybrid of them both. Washing my dirty laundry behind locked doors had got me in this whole mess.

Another dead baby. Another secret. Another sin.

And despite the joy of Connor's birth, I drove home feeling sick to my soul.

"The truth will come out," I muttered. "It will have to."

I wasn't even sure I could rely on myself any more. It was a weighty secret and one too heavy for me to carry for much longer.

# CHAPTER 22

Days later, I popped in on mum.

"Sad news," she announced. "Ellie has lost her baby."

Ellie had been due to give birth after Cath.

"That's terrible," I sympathised. "So sad."

Mum turned back to her magazine and remarked: "It was a little girl. They're burying her in Nanna Winnie's grave."

At her words, the colour was suddenly sucked from the day. Every pore in my body, from my toenail to my head, seemed to squeeze violently shut and pop open again. A shiver ripped through me so fast that I gasped.

"The same grave?" I rasped. "The same grave? Oh my god, mum. Do you realise what this means?"

Mum flicked the page over, seemingly unconcerned.

"Baby Helen is in there! They will find the remains. We're done for. I'm done for. I'll go to prison."

I babbled nonsensically as the tears rushed down my face, wet onto my clothes. Natalie and Samantha were 15 and 11 years old. I was going to prison. I would lose my children.

"Mum!" I screamed. "Listen to me!"

Mum looked at her watch and said: "We're missing *The Weakest Link*."

I had never understood whether her focus on the trivial at times of great stress was a deliberate and cynical ploy or an involuntary defence mechanism. I'd have been surprised if she knew herself. Either way, I was past caring. I needed a good lawyer, a stiff drink, a shoulder to cry on. I didn't need a talking TV Times. I left the house like a drunkard, clinging to the walls for support, hardly able to see what was in front of me. I drove home in a daze. I didn't want to tell Cath. Yet I didn't want her to hear it from mum either. Stumbling into the house, I locked the door behind me, as though that would keep out the inevitable. When I did finally pluck up courage to call Cath, my heart beat was so loud in my ears, I couldn't hear my own voice on the phone.

"Oh no!" she screamed, panic rising. "What will we do?"

Hearing the terror in Cath's voice somehow calmed me down. I realised I had to grow up, calm down and take charge. I couldn't let Cath suffer like this.

"I don't want you to have any part in this," I told her. "You were a child. Just leave it to me."

I wanted to ask her to take care of the girls, to make sure they were OK, when I went to prison. But I knew I'd break down if I even tried. And once I started crying, there would be no stopping me.

Instead, I became business like.

"I've got it all in hand, Cath," I said. "Don't you worry."

That night, I wrote a letter to my dad, explaining everything, and asking for his forgiveness.

'Looking back, I was so stupid,' I wrote. 'I did what I thought was right at the time, dad. I'm so sorry.'

I folded it into an envelope and wrote: 'In the event of my arrest' on the front. Then, with a heavy heart, I hid it in my underwear drawer.

That night, I didn't sleep at all. Instead, I crept downstairs, and googled: 'How long does it take for a body to decompose?'

And: 'Do bin bags ever rot away completely?'

As I stared at the screen, desperately scratching around for a morsel of good news, I realised my computer would soon be seized by the police and I would be damned by own search history.

"Some master criminal you are," I said scornfully.

Deeper and deeper into despair, I fell. I was tumbling into a grave full of muddy secrets. The next day, every phone call, every passing car, had me hyperventilating. I was waiting, all the time, for a knock on the door.

"I love you," I told the girls, pulling each of them close for a cuddle. "Never forget it."

# CHAPTER 23

Cath found out that the funeral was being held the following week. Neither of us planned to go. I hadn't even contacted Ellie. I couldn't bring myself to buy a sympathy card. How would that look to her when she found out the truth? I felt wretched. It's tragic enough to lose a baby, as I well knew. She would hate me when she found out what I'd done. I felt it was best to stay away from her completely.

During the night, whilst Mark and the kids were asleep, I paced the house, my mind a whirl of self-blame and self-reproach. The earth-shattering enormity of what I had done hit me, smack, for the first time. I could see it all now. So clearly. For years, I had laughed scathingly at all the men who fell for mum's sob stories and her lies. And yet I had fallen for the biggest scam of them all. She had used me to dispose of the baby's body, she had played on my own loss, knowing I was clouded by my own grief for John. I, who knew what it was to lose a child, was the perfect target, soft and wonderfully stupid. She had watched me bury her daughter, without a thought for my own safety or, even worse, for my children's. I was nothing more to her than contract waste disposal and free of charge, at that.

"What would she have done with the body, if I hadn't stepped in?" I wondered.

"Ah, but you always step in," replied my other self, a voice dripping with contempt. "You're so reliable Joanne. That's the thing with you. So reliable. So capable. So stupid."

Night after night, I tortured myself. I had nobody to confide in, no reference points. Who else could possibly advise me? I was probably, I decided, the only woman in the entire world who had buried her own sister, with her bare hands, in a public graveyard in bright sunshine. It was no badge of honour. It was bonkers. Even if I did confide in someone, I doubted they'd believe me. It was an absurd story.

And it wasn't as if, though I racked my brains, I could think of any way to ease the gravity of my situation. What was done was done. I couldn't unbury the baby. I couldn't rewind. It was too late now to go to the police, which was what I should have done at the start. In the back of my mind was a sickly suspicion that things might actually get worse than they already were. What if, for example, tests showed the baby was not stillborn? I could be an accessory to murder. Or what if mum refused to claim the baby as hers? She might land it on me or Cath. The DNA would be similar. And after all, we were younger, far more likely to fall pregnant. And to top it all, mum was such an accomplished liar. All she needed was a male police officer to flap her eyelashes at. Mentally, I raged against her. But more so, I raged against myself. Ironic. I'd been a streetwise kid, old before my time. But this, this was gullible on a grand scale. I couldn't believe I'd been so naïve.

"You're an idiot, Joanne," I told myself. "A well-meaning, top-drawer fool."

The stress was horrendous, like a ball of tinfoil wedged in my chest, growing bigger, sharper, more cumbersome, with each day that passed. I couldn't swallow it. I couldn't throw it up. And I couldn't live with it. I was stuck.

One night, I dozed off, from sheer exhaustion, but my dreams were infected with visions of Nanny Pat's monstrous Alsatian, his mouth open, his slobber dripping onto the polished parquet floor of Nanny Pat's hallway. When he got closer, I saw in horror that between his jaws, he held a tiny, helpless, baby girl.

Helen.

Blood dripped from her nose and mouth, and she was squealing pitifully from the pain where Ben's teeth had punctured and ripped her skin.

"Help!" I shouted silently. "Please someone help this baby!"

Nanny Pat clacked past us, a belligerent ghost, her shoes 50 times louder in dream land.

She shouted: "Make sure you dress that baby properly Joanne before you take it out. I won't have the neighbours saying we don't look after our own."

I ran up and down the hallway, jumping over piles of dirty washing, empty lager cans, and cat faeces, screaming for help. At the end of the passage, slumped in an armchair, showing broken, brown teeth and a swollen belly, was my mother.

"Mum!" I screamed. "It's Helen! She's needs you! This is your baby!"

But mum simply opened a magazine.

I screamed again, more loudly, and woke myself up with a jolt. I could taste vomit, and I went downstairs for a drink of water, before falling into another, tortured nightmare.

In this one, in my mind's eye, I could see a shaft of light, shining through a crack in the door. I stared, knowing, in sudden, unspeakable terror, that someone was looking back at me. There was no eye. There was no face. But it was there.

I tried to move, to wake Mark beside me, but it was as if I was drugged. I lay, leaden on the bed, immobile. I opened my mouth with a soundless, endless, scream. When I finally managed to jolt myself violently awake, I screeched so loudly that the girls came running in from their bedrooms.

"Mum!" they cried. "What's wrong?"

I was soaked with sweat, my teeth banging together.

"I'm Ok, darlings," I said shakily. "I had a silly dream."

I turned to Mark, lying next to me, and in that moment, I hated him. He had slept with my mother. He was part of everything that was wrong.

But he just rolled over onto his side and snored.

"I invoke the Middlehurst curse on you, Mark," I muttered.

# CHAPTER 24

The morning of the funeral came and I was frantic. I couldn't speak properly, even to communicate with my children. Samantha wanted help with her homework but I couldn't focus on the page.

"Let's do it tonight, after school," I mumbled.

I had never known tension like this. The day dragged. Every minute lasted an hour. I stood at the window, watching, waiting. The last day of a condemned woman. I couldn't have felt worse if I was going to the gallows.

"Come on, come on," I urged.

I knew it was coming. I just wanted it over. I didn't even go out of the house, because I didn't want to prolong the agony. I got Cath to collect the girls from school. But when she arrived home with them, at 3.30pm, I was still waiting.

"Maybe they won't find anything," Cath whispered hopefully. "Maybe, you know, if you didn't bury her deep enough, the foxes got to her. Or the rats?"

It was a disgusting, grisly notion. Yet as we recoiled at the thought, we also clung to it. Desperate for any morsel of vulgar hope. That day slowly swung round into the next. And the next. Yet there was no sense of relief, no cause for celebration. We weren't sure where the cut-off point was. After all, if they had found the remains and were testing them in a lab somewhere, the results might take weeks.

Cath and I both scoured the news for updates. We interrogated mum, as much as she would allow. But she hadn't bothered going to the funeral and she wasn't much help.

"Has anyone mentioned anything?" I pleaded. "Ellie? Your sisters? Anything at all?"

Mum shook her head dismissively. We were getting on her nerves with all our drama. She had magazines to read. Lager to drink. She was busy.

Every time I drove past the cemetery, I would steal a glance at the graves, scanning the area for those white tents and police cordons you see on TV. But there was nothing.

"Was that a good sign or not?" I wondered.

The stress showed and my weight plummeted. By the summer-time, I had dropped from a dress size 18 to a size 8. My friends all whistled approval.

"How do you do it, Joanne?" they pleaded.

"Yo-yo dieting," I said, through gritted teeth. "Runs in the family, you know."

It was a slow, slow, sort of realisation, as the months passed, that I had got away with it. This time. I didn't know how or why. But I kept my confession letter, in the drawer, just in case.

# CHAPTER 25

The stress of the baby's funeral had distracted me, for a while at least, from my troubles with Mark. But as life creaked back to some sort of uneasy normality, the rows and the tears began again.

When he was sober, Mark and I could get along just fine. We had the shared bond of our daughters and for me, they were more than enough reason to try to make our relationship work.

But when he was drunk, he was a monster. He would fly into rages so crazy that I was fearful of him. Each week, on the big shop, I had to buy him a 24 pack of Carling lager. Friday nights were strained, watching him swig from one can after another, his voice rising. Alcohol seemed to sharpen Mark up. He was more awake, more wired, more aggressive, after every drink. His exploits became part of community life, even the neighbours referred to them as 'Mark's Friday nights.' He was notorious.

It was horrible, feeling frightened in my own home. After what I had been through as a child, I wanted – needed – a safe and settled home for my own kids. And I hated myself for letting them down. They dreaded Fridays, just like I did.

And of course, with free booze on offer, my mum was never far away. She and Mark would sit and drink, bawling and cackling, until the early hours. I would lie in bed, exhausted after a hard week's work, but unable to sleep – my eye-lids stretched wide open and my ears sharp – ready to confront them if they got too close.

One night, eaten up with suspicion, I thundered downstairs to face the pair of them. Mum was all but passed out on Mark's shoulder. The audacity, the bare-faced unashamedness, enraged me.

"I know you've been having sex!" I shrieked. "You're sleeping with my mother!"

Mark shook his head and got to his feet, ready for a row. But I was in no mood to back down. My chest was thumping with the injustice of it all.

"Do you know, she had a baby?" I spat. "Your baby no doubt. I buried your bloody baby, Mark. And one day, the truth will come out."

The colour drained from his face and I knew I had gone too far. The idea had been lurking around, in a marshy part of my mind, that Mark might be Helen's father. It seemed unbelievable, yet logical, all at once. Yet this was the first time I had dared to voice it.

"Piss off!" he shouted. "You're sick! You don't know what you're saying."

"You're sick!" I retorted. "That baby would be the girls' aunty and their half-sister! My half-sister and my step-daughter! Now surely that's sick!"

I stamped off to bed, still seething, my mind whirling. It was entirely possible that Mark had fathered that baby. I had lain next to him in bed, for years, torturing myself about that poor little girl. What if she was his? What if I had risked everything – to save his skin too? The irony was so sour that I gagged on it.

The following morning, mum was splayed out on a couch, Mark was slumped in an armchair. Both were unconscious. I clattered around them, cleaning ashtrays and the abhorrent Carling cans, as noisily as I could. Then, I flicked the hoover on. I was steaming. I could almost feel the clouds of anger fizzing from me.

I waited for Mark to flicker an eye-lid and then I was there, inches from his face, on with my tirade.

"You're a disgrace!" I bellowed, spittle flying from my lips like it was turbo-powered.

I jerked my head to where mum was snoring like a walrus behind me.

"You're having sex with her! Now that's the best mother-in-law joke I ever heard!" I only reined myself in when I heard the girls on the stairs. My heart sank. I had always tried – and believed I'd succeeded – to protect them from the worst of the nastiness between me and Mark.

But Samantha walked past me, into the kitchen, with her head down.

"I'm sorry," I told her. "I really am, please don't listen to me and dad. We're just being silly."

"How can you say that about him?" she asked.

Her big eyes were full of reproach and sadness and a piece of my heart was chipped away.

Natalie was a different prospect. She was older, more mature. And she was nosey, too. Where Samantha preferred not to know, she was anxious for every detail.

"Why don't you leave him, mum?" she asked. "He'll never change. You know that."

I nodded wearily.

"I should," I told her. "I really should."

Instead, I tried short-term measures. I got temazepam sleeping tablets from Mark's mum and, using two teaspoons, I crushed them into granules. Then, half-way through Mark's next bender, I slipped them into his lager. It was gratifying – fabulous even – to watch him suddenly slur and roll his eyes, before collapsing in a heap on the rug. I didn't even bring him a blanket. I hoped he'd freeze to death.

"Sweet dreams," I smiled.

And I flicked off the light and went to bed.

The tablets worked well for a time. But when he woke the next day, he was still fuzzy with the drugs, and I worried he might suspect something. I knew I had to be careful. Besides, I didn't have a never-ending supply of sedatives. I was a housewife, not a drug-dealer, and I hadn't a clue how to go about acquiring any more.

# CHAPTER 26

In Autumn 2006, I began to suspect that Mark was seeing someone else behind my back. I noticed he was showering every night both before and after his trips to the pub, which was unheard of for him. But I said nothing. I couldn't face the argument. Besides, it was quite a relief that he was out all the time. I liked having the house to myself, with the girls. The peace was welcome.

"Mum you must promise me that you'll leave him," Natalie said to me. "You deserve so much better."

She knew I would never break a promise to her. And I also knew she was only doing this for my own good.

"By January next year, I will have it sorted," I vowed.

One night, Mark was out at the pub, when the computer flashed with an MSN message. I realised he'd left his account logged on. Intrigued, I clicked on the little blue icon.

"It really turned me on when you came round like that the other night," winked the message.

My eyes widened. It was from a woman. And from a woman I knew too! It didn't take more than a quick scan of the recent history to realise they were having an affair. But there was no jealousy, no hurt. I was way past all that. Instead, I felt a little thrill of mischief.

"Can't wait to see you again," I wrote. "Baby, I miss you."

Mark was no romantic. And so, if I was going to get rid of him, this was my chance. I would seduce her myself, on his behalf! I quickly deleted the message and said nothing to him. But a few nights later, when he was out again, I sent her another love message; careful not to overdo it so that he twigged, but enough to keep the sap rising.

"She'll welcome you with open arms," I sniggered, logging off his account.

A couple of days later, my phone rang at work, and it was Mark's mate, Tom. I was the manager of a tail-lift company and busy going through a pile of orders when he called.

"Oh, hi," I said in surprise. "I didn't even know you knew where I worked."

There was a silence, and then he said: "I wondered if you fancied a drink this weekend?"

"Oh, um, I'll ask Mark and get back to you," I replied, slightly irritated that he was calling me at work for something so trivial.

I hung up, went back to my work, and the phone rang again. And again, it was Tom.

"Actually," he blurted. "I didn't mean Mark. I want to go for a drink with you, on your own."

His voice shook a little and my heart skipped a beat as I realised what he was saying.

"Have you been drinking?" I demanded.

But it was early afternoon and I knew Tom was not a drinker. He didn't sound drunk either.

"No," he replied sheepishly. "I'd just like to see you."

Immediately, alarm bells rang. This was a set-up by Mark. I was sure of it. He had found out about my messages on MSN. And this was his revenge for me sending saucy love-notes to his fancy piece.

"Let me think about it," I said to Tom, hoping to sound non-committal. "I'll get back to you."

That night, I watched Mark closely. But he was no different from usual. He showered before going out – presumably to see his girlfriend – and he showered when he got home. He went to bed with a grunt and barely made eye contact.

I was perplexed. Usually, if Mark was up to something, I could spot it a million miles away. He was not a man capable of complex deception. But he seemed perfectly normal. I let a few more days go by, and I began to think I was wrong. Perhaps this wasn't a prank after all. Tom called me again at work, and this time, without really thinking too deeply, I agreed to meet him for a drink.

Cath agreed to have the girls overnight as Mark insisted he couldn't miss his regular snooker. I made a silent joke about ball games and his secret girlfriend and waited until he had left before I got ready. I felt strangely guilty. And yet, there was no reason. I was meeting a friend for a drink and that was that. Even so, I chose a flattering red summer dress, with white sandals, and I took care over my make-up.

Tom arrived on time, as promised, and as I spotted his car, I felt a frisson of excitement, followed by confusion. We drove to a pub far from anyone we knew.

"What's all this about?" I asked, sipping on a diet coke.

I was still half-expecting Mark to walk in and gloat over the elaborate set-up. But instead, Tom gulped. "I've fancied you for a long time," he said nervously, his fingers drumming the table. "I thought you knew."

"What?" I shrieked, choking on an ice-cube. "Are you serious? Can you imagine what Mark would say? We're still together, you know."

Tom shrugged.

"He doesn't deserve you," he said.

"Well, you're right there," I laughed.

I was amazed, and secretly pleased, to think that someone else had noticed. There were so many days when I had felt as though I was wading through cold custard, on my own, with no one to care about me.

It seemed I had been wrong.

I had never really thought of Tom in that way before. Maybe, just maybe, I should start to do so…

# CHAPTER 27

Tom rang me again the following day, and I blushed when I heard his voice.

"I wanted to apologise for shocking you last night," he said. "I really though you would have guessed. I didn't realise it was going to be such a big surprise."

"It's fine," I said, suddenly shy and a little giggly. "It was nice in a way. I really enjoyed our drink together."

We arranged to meet up again that night.

"How've you been?" he asked, as I got into the car. "I've been worried I might have scared you off."

I grinned.

"I'm made of tougher stuff than that," I replied.

Already, I had a mental checklist running, him in one column, Mark in another.

Again, we talked for ages. And again, nothing happened. But I felt myself warming to Tom, melting. He was softly-spoken, easy-going and kind-hearted. He was interested in me – and that counted for a lot. I couldn't remember the last time Mark had paid me any compliments or showed me any attention. I wasn't used to this. But could I get used to this?

"I really admire you," Tom told me.

The flattery was lovely. I was so sick of years upon years of Mark drinking, shouting, spending all our money. I wanted a new start.

Mark had already moved on – his MSN account was bubbling with sex and sauce, thanks to me. I dropped his girlfriend another flirty message before I went to bed that night. She and Mark seemed to have no idea that I was helping their relationship along, and it made me chuckle when I thought of it. I felt no malice at all towards her. In fact, I wished her all the luck in the world.

"You'll certainly need it, love," I thought, as I switched off the computer.

A few weeks later, I was invited out with the girls from work and it gave me an excuse to be out overnight.

"I'm going out in town and we're all staying over at one of the girl's places," I told Mark. "I won't be back until tomorrow."

The night went ahead as planned. But afterwards, I had arranged to meet Tom at a friend's house. She was away and had given me the keys. Seeing him waiting for me, on the street outside, gave me a rush of excitement.

"Let's get inside," I smiled. "I can't wait."

It had been a slow burner. Those dates, night after night, where we had only talked and laughed together, had been the build-up to this. Tom knew how to stoke a fire, I had to give him that. And now, suddenly, it felt like all bets were off and I couldn't keep my hands off him. We fell into each other's arms in the hallway. I kicked off my shoes and Tom carried me upstairs.

We were wrapped around each other, stark naked, when suddenly there was a knock at the door. Tom and I froze, the passion draining from us. I crept to the bedroom window and peered out into the street below.

"Bloody hell, Tom!" I whispered. "Mark's car is outside. He's here."

Next came another loud rap at the door. I peeped out again and to my astonishment, I spotted a woman in the passenger seat.

"Mark has brought his girlfriend here to catch us out," I squeaked. "The bloody cheek of him! Talk about double standards!"

It was outrageously funny. But I was scared stiff, too. I didn't know whether to laugh or scream. The door banged again and I jumped.

My shoes, distinctive strappy stilettoes, were at the bottom of the stairs. If Mark so much as peeped through the letterbox, I'd had it.

We both held our breath as, mercifully, the knocking stopped, Mark swore loudly, we heard a car door slam, an engine rev, and then he drove away, tyres screeching.

"That was close," I gulped, pulling the quilt up over my head. "Very close."

The next morning, I was home early, bracing myself for a showdown. But to my surprise, Mark was still in bed, and he said nothing when he got up. It wasn't like him to play mind games. I didn't know what was going on.

A couple of days later, I was busy at work, when he called. And this time, I was left in no doubt.

"Get home now!" he bawled. "And I mean now!"

My stomach did a half turn. I hung up and called Tom.

"He knows," I said.

I was all jittery and clammy. I was dreading facing Mark, but I knew it had to be done. Driving home, I didn't feel an ounce of guilt or remorse. Of course, there was a sadness. We'd had three precious children together. He had been my first love. I thought back to that first night, me plastered in Julie's mum's make-up, him leading me down the ginnel for our first kiss. And despite everything, I smiled. The memory was lovely.

I had tried hard to make our relationship work. More than anything, I had wanted a nice home for our daughters, with a mum and dad who loved each other. I certainly hadn't wanted us to end up hating each other.

Now, as the final nail was being hammered in, I didn't even have the energy to pick another fight.

"I know you're having an affair!" Mark shouted.

I didn't know how he knew and I didn't ask. I just shook my head in denial. I was too frightened of the consequences.

Now he was towering over me, his eyes wild and his whole body shaking with fury, those moments down the ginnel seemed very long ago.

"You've got it all wrong," I stammered.

Mark's eyes were still hard with menace and I decided to take a different tack.

"I know all about your girlfriend," I told him. "I know who she is. I know you see her every night. It's over between us Mark. You know that just as much as I do," I sighed, heavily. "I want you to move out. But I hope you're happy together. I really do."

Mark snarled. He thought I was being sarcastic but I genuinely meant every word. Still, any happiness seemed a long way away.

"I am not moving out," he vowed. "And you can't make me."

We had two months of rows, leading up to Christmas and out of the other side. There were tears, tantrums and trauma, all through the festive period, until I was weary and desperate for it to end.

Early in January 2007, I was conscious that the deadline I had set with Natalie was fast approaching.

"Enough is enough," I said. "Today is the day."

I called my mum and asked her to come round.

"You know Mark better than I do," I said to her. "I need you to back me up. I want him to leave."

I didn't say: "You've slept with him more than I have, too," but that was the sub-text and we both knew it.

It was a sordid situation, but I had decided to use it to my advantage. "If you can't beat 'em, join 'em, Joanne," I told myself.

And my hunch paid off. Mark had ignored my demands and pleas for months. But with my mother stood next to me, he seemed to suddenly shrink.

"You need to do as Joanne says," mum said, rather flatly, but she said it at least.

I was annoyed that it hurt me still how much of a hold she had over him. He was like putty.

Mum and I had an awkward cup of tea while Mark went upstairs to pack his bags. Not long after, the front door banged, and he was gone.

"Well, you've managed something I couldn't," I said to mum.

I couldn't quite bring myself to thank her. But it was a good job done. After 19 years, Mark was finally out of my hair.

"Just like you promised," Nat smiled. "I'm proud of you, mum."

I made a resolution never to buy another can of Carling for the rest of my life. Even seeing them in the supermarket gave me vivid flashbacks. But I felt lighter and younger, without Mark around. And I was enjoying my relationship with Tom, too. I felt more alive than I had for years.

In the office, my workmates took to wafting their hands above my head.

"Just brushing away those love hearts, Joa," they joked.

I was usually a quite contained, measured person. But those days, I wore a smile as wide as the Mersey tunnel. I was smitten and I didn't care who knew it.

It wasn't full-on and serious. I wasn't ready for that. We'd see each other maybe three times a week. And I grew to really like the arrangement. It was lovely to see Tom, but it was also good to have nights on my own too, with the girls.

I loved those nights when I could slob out, in my pyjamas, with a full bar of chocolate to myself, safe in the knowledge I didn't need to shave my legs, wash my hair or suck my stomach in.

Part-time love suited me perfectly.

And those snatched moments and last-minute dates just made our time together so much more special.

Yet I had cheated on Mark and it was wrong and I had enough decency to feel ashamed. It wasn't lost on me that my mother had cheated on Karl. Was I more like her than I cared – or dared – to admit? It was a disturbing thought and my happiness curdled a little. I buried the thought as quickly as it surfaced.

My moral compass was spiralling. But, for once, I vowed not to care. I had spent my whole life being responsible and thinking of others. I had been all grown up and careworn even by the time I started school. This was just a bit of fun. My bit of fun. And I didn't see what was wrong with that.

# CHAPTER 28

At first, I confided only in Julie, my oldest friend. But then, as we got more serious, I realised I should tell Cath and the girls, too.

Natalie took it well.

"You deserve some happiness, mum," she said warmly.

Cath, too, was pleased although there was a note of caution in her voice.

"You haven't had the best of luck with men," she said. "Just make sure he's right for you, Joa. Don't get hurt again."

I brushed her advice away with a laugh. I was the grown up, after all. I was the one in charge of dishing out advice. Cath, no matter how old she got, would always be my baby sis.

She hugged me as I left and there was one thing I was certain of. Men could come and go – as they certainly always do. But nothing would ever come between Cath and me.

Driving home, I knew Samantha would be something of a challenge, and that night, I cooked her a shepherd's pie as a bribe. Over dinner, I blurted it out.

"I've got a new boyfriend," I told her. "I've been seeing him for a while. I'll be honest, I was seeing him whilst me and your dad were still together."

"What?" Samantha hissed.

The disgust was dripping off the end of her fork. She dropped her cutlery and spat each word, like it pained her.

"How could you?"

I knew it was hard for her, because she loved her dad dearly. I tried to be patient. But Samantha, in a teenage strop, abandoned her dinner and slammed out of the room. She banged the door with such force that the whole house shook.

"Give her time," I told myself.

But the weeks passed and Samantha did not seem to mellow. Tom came round to officially meet her, but she was rude and off-hand. She rarely spoke to him. I remembered my own treatment of Karl, when he first moved in with me and mum, and I couldn't help but smile.

"Like it or not," I told her, as she slammed yet another door. "You're a chip off the old block."

# CHAPTER 29

At the end of 2007, I decided to move house. Then Cath discovered she was pregnant with her third baby, and she began looking for a bigger house. Finally, co-incidentally, mum announced she was moving too.

"I've never settled here," she said vaguely. "I want somewhere new."

"All three of us at the same time," I groaned. "This will be fun."

I knew we'd have to help mum pack and move, although it would be nothing like as bad as last time. We roped Chris in to help.

Mum's moving day dawned and I busied myself in the kitchen, picking through piles of rubbish and filling countless bin bags. Then Cath, who had been clearing mum's bedroom, suddenly appeared at my shoulder.

"I found the red bin," she whispered. "It's still there, in her wardrobe."

My blood ran cold. The red bin. It was like ripping open an old scar. Not again, I groaned inwardly. I felt a mixture of fear and fury. Why the hell hadn't mum thrown it away? What use could it possibly serve now?

Cath explained that as soon as she'd spotted the bin, mum had run across the room at her and slammed the wardrobe door shut.

"I haven't seen her run so fast for years," Cath said quietly, her voice wobbly. "There's something in that bin. I'm sure of it."

We both went into the bedroom where mum was casually throwing her clothes into a bin bag, her face blank.

"What's in that red bin?" Cath asked loudly.

"Books," she snapped. "Now leave it."

We watched as she lifted the bin from the wardrobe and placed it with the rest of her belongings. There was no reason to doubt her. After all, what else could be in there? But I felt sick and uneasy. And I knew Cath felt the same. Troubled, we went back into mum's bedroom to dismantle the bed. But, as we lifted the mattress, a blob of wriggling, glistening maggots fell from one end, and we both stared in disgust. Cath ran from the room, retching.

I stared at the maggots. I thought of the red bin. And I was gripped with a cold dread.

"Pull yourself together, Joanne," I snapped. "Come on."

By the time we were ready to load the van, it was dark outside.

"You take a breather," I said to mum and Cath. "Chris and I will do the heavy lifting."

As we emptied the house, I kept my eye on the red bin. And I made sure it was still there, hidden behind a curtain, as we drove away from the house for the last time.

"We'll go back later and have a look inside," I whispered to Cath.

She nodded.

"I think we need to tell Chris as well," she replied. "He has a right to know."

I didn't want to tell Chris. But she was right. We couldn't keep him out of this any longer.

It was about 10pm by the time we got mum settled in for the evening.

"We've a couple more things to drop off for you," I told her. "We'll see you later. Or maybe tomorrow. Let's see how we get on."

Back in the van, the three of us sat in silence. Cath and I were so uptight that Chris could feel it.

"What's going on?" he demanded.

I hesitated. I had carried this secret around for so long. I had longed to confide in someone, other than Cath. Yet now the time had to come to share it, I couldn't do it.

Where to start?

"Mum had a stillborn baby," Cath said matter-of-factly. "She kept it in a red bin until Joa buried it for her. We've found the red bin again today and mum's reaction has got us worried."

I could tell Chris didn't believe a word of it. He was, by nature, extremely laid-back and tolerant, though this was pushing it, even for him. Quietly, I filled in the details; how I had dug a grave with my bare hands and how I had driven myself half-insane with grief and shame and worry ever since.

As I spoke, I could feel the dirt under my nails again. I could hear the hum of quiet conversation in the cemetery around me. And I could smell it. God I could smell it again.

Chris pursed his lips. He believed us now.

"We need to open the bin," he said eventually.

Cath and I nodded and we drove, giddy with panic, back to the old house. But by now, the electric was off and the place was in darkness. We flicked the torches on our mobile phones and went inside. It was eerie and deathly quiet. The three of us stood inside the door of the living room, momentarily frozen.

"I don't know about this," Cath stuttered.

Her voice was jittery and scared. Even Chris, in the half-light, looked ill-at-ease.

"I'll do it," I said.

I didn't want to. But I was the eldest. I had a responsibility. Striding over to the window, as though I was confronting a school bully, I yanked the bin into the middle of the room.

"Ready," I breathed.

My stomach felt like it was going to fall right through me. I lifted the lid, my eyes and mouth clamped shut, half-expecting a swarm of locusts to fly out.

Chris peered inside.

"Well, it's not books," he said grimly.

He was right. There were what seemed to be layers of black bin bags, with five or six throwaway air fresheners on the top. The insides of the air fresheners were withered and dry; they had clearly been there for a long time. And the edges of the bin bags, though not wet, looked sticky and sweaty.

"Let's leave it," I said suddenly, and I clanged the lid back on.

I was surprised to hear myself say it. I had fully intended to see this through. But now, I knew, I just couldn't. Whatever it was, it was too much. It was going too far.

Chris was put out, I could see that.

"I want to look," he insisted. "I'll do it."

But I was firm. I was already implicated in the death of one baby. I didn't want Chris and Cath dragged into this too. Whether it was raging fear or logical self-preservation, or a mix of both, I didn't know.

"Come on," I said. "Let's get this into the van."

There were a couple more bin bags of stuff. And we took the lot, straightaway, to mum's new house. I made a point of carrying the red bin right into the middle of her living room, where she was sitting in an armchair. And then, with the toe of my boot, I kicked it over.

Mum shot out of her chair as though she'd been stung and reached the bin almost as soon as it fell. She glared at me as she banged the lid back into place.

"Be more careful," she hissed.

It was good advice. Especially after my previous carelessness, in the graveyard. I certainly didn't intend to repeat that. Back in the van, as we drove away, Chris was still adamant that we should have looked inside the bin.

"Once you've looked, there may be no going back," I told him.

This time, I had to think of my family. What if there was another baby? The idea was preposterous. Yet she had done it once. I couldn't take that risk.

"If the police and social services get involved, I'll be in a whole shit-load of trouble," I told Chris. "And so would Cath. And you. Just forget about the bin. Bury it."

It was a poor choice of words. But it was what we needed to do.

# Chapter 30

In my mind, I felt absolutely sure that the truth about Helen would eventually come out. My only hope was to push the inevitable as far into the future as I could – until my girls were older. It was like starting a diet. Always tomorrow. But if I had to go to prison, I was determined to make sure first that they were OK.

And as for the red bin, I was, at times, absolutely certain that there was another baby in there. Yet I was also equally desperate for that not to be so. Much of it, I realised, was denial. I had buried one baby. I could not do it again. I was petrified.

On good days, I could convince myself that it was just a pile of old rubbish in there. After all, mum's house was full of rotten bin bags. This was just the same. And there was no smell, not like the last time. The red bin didn't smell one bit. Surely, nobody – not even her – could repeat the horror show of Helen's birth and death.

But why the air-fresheners? And why was she so cagey about the bin? I remembered the way she had snapped at Cath. The way she had lunged across the room after I kicked the bin over. She was more protective over the bloody bin than she was over her own children, I thought bitterly. Or was it all one and the same?

The argument raced round and round my head for months and then years. I was never free of it. The red bin was like a sinister spectre, hovering over me. I might not be behind bars. But I would never be free.

There was something, someone, in there.

Cath, Chris and I had endless, fruitless discussions. The worry, the uncertainty, was all-consuming.

"If there is another baby, she must have been pregnant," I said. "But when?"

I thought back to the large blood stain, on the bedroom carpet and I felt suddenly queasy. Was it a nosebleed? Or had she just given birth? The idea was so preposterous. I didn't know what to think.

One night, Cath arrived armed with a load of photos she'd gathered together over the years.

"I've dug out all the family photos I can find," she said. "I wondered if we might spot something. A baby bump. Swollen ankles maybe?"

It was difficult. Mum wore shapeless, baggy clothes all the time, so she could have been pregnant in virtually every picture. Or maybe she was just, as she had always said, a yo-yo dieter.

And there was the issue of the father. Mum had had boyfriends, nobody too serious. And of course, there was Mark. I shuddered at the thought. I couldn't voice it to Cath or Chris. But he was number one suspect on my list.

"But why would she risk getting pregnant again, after Helen?" I reasoned. "Why wouldn't she use contraception, or have an abortion?"

Cath shivered.

"Maybe she gets pregnant on purpose," she suggested weakly. "You know, like some sort of depraved addiction."

I gulped. Did she get a twisted kick out of getting pregnant? Was this her thing? Like other people did extreme sports, did she do extreme pregnancies?

Or maybe she liked being pregnant because it was a way of feeling close to someone. She had never, as far as I knew, been close to her own parents or her siblings. She certainly had never bonded with her own children.

Did she bond with unborn babies?

The problem was, every time we talked, it raised more questions than answers.

One night, Natalie's face appeared at the living room door, as Cath and I were writing out a timeline of mum's relationships.

"We need to tell you something, Joa," Cath said, a little anxiously. "Natalie knows about Helen. I told her. Years ago."

I stared from one to the other – aghast.

"You promised!" I shrieked. "How could you, Cath?"

But even as I spoke, I forgave her. Cath had been a young teenager when I buried the baby. How could I have expected her to carry the secret around, for so many years, all by herself?

As Natalie had grown up, she and Cath had become close. As Cath and I were like mum and daughter, Cath and Nat were like sisters. It was inevitable they would share secrets.

"Well, at least you confided in someone who wouldn't go to the police," I smiled eventually. "It's in her interest to have me around I suppose."

"I confided in someone who I knew would believe me and support me," Cath said warmly. "Natalie knows what lengths you would go to for us all, Joa. Don't ever think we don't appreciate it."

# CHAPTER 31

One evening, after a long day at work, I rushed home for a quick bath before going out with Cath. But when I got there, Natalie was already up to her neck in bubbles.

"Come on, Nat," I wheedled. "I've got to meet Aunty Cath, I need the bath!"

But she fixed me with frightened eyes and said: "Mum, I have something to tell you."

Immediately, I knew.

"You're not pregnant, are you?" I asked.

She dropped her gaze and nodded.

"Oh, Nat," I sighed sadly.

She was only seventeen. She had just got a good job working in an office. Her future was bursting with possibility.

"It's your decision," I said. "If you want a termination, it will stay between you and me. I'll support you – no matter what."

205

And as I spoke, I realised that was what mattered most of all. Support. In her position, I'd been given nothing. Not even a headstone for my dead baby. It would be different for my daughter.

Of course I couldn't pretend I wasn't upset, disappointed. This wasn't what I had planned. I had frogmarched her to the GP myself for the contraceptive pill. I had drummed the importance of safe sex into her. I'd been so determined that she wouldn't be a young mum, like I was.

But once again, my determination to get rid of the past had backfired spectacularly and here it was, right slap bang in the middle of my life again.

"I'm keeping the baby," she told me. "I've made up my mind."

We made an appointment with the GP and afterwards I attended every scan, every ante-natal check. At her 20-week scan, she discovered she was having a little girl.

"Not another girl!" I joked.

Cath announced she and her husband, John, were expecting again too, and, with two sons already, she was hoping for a daughter. When her scan showed she was carrying a boy, we all dissolved into giggles.

"You should swap, after the birth," I joked.

Towards the end of the pregnancy, Natalie and her boyfriend got a flat together. We all painted and decorated every room, until it was ready. And now, the anticipation built. And built.

CHAPTER 31

This was my first grandchild and I was just about ready to pop myself with the excitement of it all. Late at night, on June 13 2008, Natalie called me to say she was in labour.

"I'm on my way," I said.

I arrived at her flat, and insisted she put on her coat and shoes, ready for a stroll.

"Why?" she groaned. "I just want to lie down mum, please."

I shook my head.

"Walking will bring the labour on," I told her. "Come on, let's get cracking."

We walked slowly around the streets, arm in arm. Occasionally, Natalie would drop to the pavement, yelping in pain, as a contraction took hold. I carried a towel, to slip under her knees, every time she went down.

Afterwards, I drove her to hospital. I was there to see my gorgeous granddaughter, Kiera, born at 10.30am the following morning, and weighing 7lbs 14ozs.

As she was laid on Natalie's chest, I felt a rush of love and gratitude. Baby Kiera turned her head a little and looked at me intently.

"She knows who I am!" I gushed proudly. "She likes me!"

It was the beginning of a beautiful bond. I looked after Kiera every Saturday night, and many times in-between. I spoiled her with dresses, stripy tights and toys. She and I were inseparable. I called her my 'sweetie-pie'. And her name for me, when she began to talk, was "Mum Pie."

In August, Cath had a little boy, Aaron.

Two beautiful, bouncing, babies in the family gave us a reason to smile. Cath and Natalie spent more and time together, at baby massage and coffee mornings. It was good to see that bond being continued and passed on. Our family had been rotten at the core. But the new seeds, the new generation, were pure and positive.

And I loved looking after little Kiera, her face next to mine as I sang to her. She smelled so innocent, so fresh. But sometimes, as I breathed in her newness, I was suddenly slammed right back to the scene at the grave. The dirty brown bag, the clots of foetal blood, the putrid smell of decomposing flesh.

Would I be haunted by this forever? And yet if this was my only punishment, I would surely be grateful. For bizarrely, as time went on, it seemed more likely – not less – that I would pay for this in prison.

# CHAPTER 32

By August 2009, mum was in arrears with her rent and she was facing eviction. Yet again, she needed to move house quickly. But this time, she had nowhere to go. I knew she was stressed. Her health wasn't good either; she had trouble with her breathing and she had been diagnosed with COPD.

"I'll do what I can to help," I promised her.

Again, I wondered why on earth I was looking after a mother who had never looked after me.

One Friday night, I was soaking in the bath after work and I heard the phone ring.

"Mum, it's Chris!" Natalie shouted. "It's urgent."

Cursing, I climbed out, grabbed a towel, and raced downstairs to the phone.

"I can't wake mum up," Chris told me. "She's left a note saying she can't carry on. She's had enough."

Chris sounded like his usual laid-back self but I was immediately concerned.

"I'm on my way," I said.

Natalie and I jumped in the car and I called Cath on the way. She arranged to meet us there. We arrived almost at the same time and rushed into the hallway.

"She's upstairs," Chris said. "No response."

I dashed into the bedroom and felt mum's pulse.

"She's alive," I said, noticing empty blister packs of paracetamol at the side of the bed.

"So," said Cath, in a strange voice. "What do we do now?"

"Well," I replied, my voice equally strange. "I really don't know."

A wicked thought flitted in, and straight out, of my mind.

"I'll call an ambulance," I said, defeatedly.

Whilst we waited for the paramedics, I stood by mum's bedside, and I saw her eyes flicker once or twice.

"I don't think she's quite as sick as she's making out," I said to Cath grimly.

This was typical of mum. More mind games. No doubt this was all connected to her rent arrears. The ambulance arrived and after an assessment, the paramedic said: "I know you can hear me Bernadette."

But she didn't respond at all. And so, mum was lifted onto a stretcher and taken off to hospital. Cath and I followed. She was transferred onto a ward and we were told she might be kept in a couple of days, for tests. But there was no great sense of urgency.

"I'm off home," I said, even though mum still hadn't opened her eyes. "I'll bring some clothes in for you tomorrow."

The next morning, I called at her house. I was in a rush, irritable that I had to fit a hospital visit into my already busy day at work. It was all about her – again. It was incredible how she managed to make herself the centre of attention of every occasion. Flinging open the doors of her double wardrobe, I sighed as a pile of magazines, shoes and clothes tumbled out.

"Typical," I muttered.

I stooped to catch a pair of shoes as they fell. Then, as I shoved them back, I caught sight of the red bin, hidden behind all the mess.

My breath spasmed. I was all alone. And I was very afraid.

With my blood pumping, I dragged the bin out onto the carpet, and before I could think too deeply, I lifted the lid. Inside, there were two tea towels, folded in layers, layer upon layer of lies. Gingerly, I moved them away, and underneath, it was just the same as it had been two years earlier, the tacky, glistening, bin bags and the shrunken old air-fresheners.

I willed myself to lift the bin-bags, to look underneath. But I just couldn't do it. Screaming in frustration, at my own cowardice, I slammed the lid back and pushed the bin back into the wardrobe. Sighing in annoyance, I grabbed some clean underwear, a jumper and a pair of trousers, and set off for the hospital.

On my way, I called Cath.

"I found the bloody bin again," I told her, my voice cracked with stress and anger. "I can't carry on like this."

Cath met me at the hospital. We marched onto mum's ward and it was all I could do to stop myself throwing the clothes at her. I was furious. I didn't even ask her how she was. I didn't want to hear the lies. I was angry about the 'overdose'. Angry about the red bin. Angry that she was my mother.

Outside the hospital, I said to Cath: "I think she should speak to Dish. This has gone on long enough."

"I'm coming with you," Cath said.

We called Chris and he wanted to come too. Dish was a social worker, and I thought she was the most reasonable of mum's siblings. She lived in a bungalow, opposite Nanny Pat's old house. The place was in darkness, and it looked sad and forlorn. We knocked on Dish's door and she welcomed us inside. Her friend, Jane, made us tea and brought biscuits. But I couldn't even swallow, let alone chew a biscuit.

"I think mum has problems," I began. "She gave birth to a baby, a stillborn baby, and I buried it in Nanna Winnie's grave."

Dish's face remained calm, blank, throughout.

"I'll talk to her," she promised.

The following day, mum was discharged from hospital. I plonked her hospital bag down in the hallway and she turned to me.

"I'm going to the cinema tonight," she announced. "I'm going out with Dish. Do you fancy it?"

Numbly, I shook my head. She had only been out of hospital for a matter of minutes – and instead of talking to her about babies and bins, her sister was taking her out on the town! It seemed as though the whole world was going mad around me. The days passed and I heard nothing. And I realised, with a crushing sense of disappointment, that Dish couldn't help me.

"Maybe she didn't believe us," Cath said. "To be honest, Joa, you did sound crazy when you were speaking to her. I wouldn't blame her for thinking you were a compulsive liar."

I shrugged, helpless. I felt like I was sinking deeper and deeper into a bottomless pit, where every avenue of help, every promise of sanity, turned out to be a bigger problem than the problem itself.

That same week, on the Friday, I was going to an Ann Summer's naughty knickers party, with my mate, Julie. She had arranged to pick me up and, by now, I felt like a pressure cooker, whistling towards boiling point. I was ready to pop. The party really was the last thing I felt like doing. But I was in so much of a dither, I couldn't think of an excuse to pull out, at this late stage. It just seemed easier to go along. Besides, I'd promised to go. I didn't like letting people down, especially not Julie.

But as soon as she knocked on my door, I felt a rising tide of panic.

"What's the matter?" she asked. "You don't look well."

"I'm alright," I breathed, grabbing my handbag. "Let's just get going."

The party was being held by one of Julie's mates in a small terraced house in St Helens. The room was full of women I knew, hooting with laughter as they waved sex

213

aids in the air and strutted around in baby doll nighties and fishnets.

The drink flowed, the music blared and one woman got up to dance with a pair of crotchless knickers on her head.

I'd usually have been in my element. But tonight, I felt cold and removed. I knocked back three or four vodkas, but I felt stubbornly sober. I knew I could drink all night without getting drunk. My head was whirring. The constant worry was exhausting, it was wearing me out. Desperate to get away from the noise, I slunk out into the garden for a while and Julie followed.

"What's up?" she pressed. "Is it the girls? Sam or Nat? Have you fallen out?"

I shook my head.

"Nothing like that," I whispered.

To my dismay, I started to cry and Julie took my arm.

"We need to get out of here," she said quietly. "Come on."

We left the party early, me mumbling excuses about a migraine, and went straight back to my house. In the taxi, on the way there, I made a decision.

No more secrets.

I had once thought it would kill me if the truth came out. Now, I realised, it would kill me if it didn't.

"It's my mum," I said to Julie. "I need to talk to you."

First, I knew I had to speak to Cath.

"No!" Cath yelled when I phoned. "Don't tell her. Don't tell anyone, Joa. It will cause so much trouble."

214

I understood. She was more scared for me than for herself. But I could hear my dad's voice, clearly, in my head.

"Right and wrong, Joanne," he would have said. "Always do the right thing."

For years, I'd consoled myself that the lines were blurred. That it was difficult to separate the two. But now I saw, perhaps for the first time, that there was one choice. The right choice. And I had to be strong enough to make it.

I opened the front door, and by now Julie was bursting with impatience.

"What's your mum done now?" she demanded. "What the hell has she done?"

Samantha was in the living room and I realised that she needed to know, too.

I held my head in my hands, and it all spilled out. Once I started talking, I couldn't stop. The floodgates had opened. I told them everything.

"Mum," Samantha gasped. "I am so sorry. I didn't know you were going through this. No wonder you gave dad and Bernie a hard time."

Julie listened, open mouthed, tears streaming down her cheeks.

"I always knew how bad your mum was," she wept. "But this is unbelievable. I don't know how you've carried this around. I really don't."

It was a comfort that they didn't blame me or hate me for what I had done. But I knew Julie was thinking ahead, and she was frightened for me.

"We should go and talk to my mum," she said eventually. "She'll know what to do."

Pat was the kind soul who had made me egg sandwiches and a hot brew before school every morning. She had tried to look after me, Cath and Chris, the best she could, when we were neighbours. Nowadays, she ran support groups for families fleeing domestic violence. More than anything else, she was sensible, logical, normal. Every day qualities, but they were in scarce supply in my world.

# CHAPTER 33

Pat had moved house since we were kids, and it was a relief not to have to drive down my old street, past the house of horrors where I'd once lived.

"This is a nice surprise," Pat smiled, as she opened the front door.

It was past midnight, and she was in a dressing gown. Apart from the hallway light, the house was in darkness.

"I'm sorry to get you up," I said lamely.

I was shivering, even though it wasn't cold. Julie had called to warn her we were coming, and I felt sure she must have briefed her. But if she had, Pat didn't give anything away. When we were children, she'd always been strict, but unfailingly fair and kind. Pat was a single mum, she'd escaped an unhappy relationship herself, and she had struggled. But despite her own issues, she was a good, loving mum, who fed and clothed not only her own kids, but me as well. The memory of those early morning butties had stayed with me, right through to adulthood. I thought of Pat, with an overwhelming sense of gratitude, every time I fried an egg.

Pat's home was, as I would have expected, well-worn but welcoming. Julie and I sat side by side on the couch.

"Tell her," Julie babbled. "Tell her!"

"Shut up, Julie," Pat said sharply. "Give her time."

My mouth was dry, as though I'd been eating gravel. My head down, my hands clasped between my knees, I took a deep breath.

"Mum had a baby which didn't survive and I buried it for her," I said, almost shamefully. "I thought I was doing the right thing. I really did."

I couldn't look at Pat. I couldn't bear to see judgement, or worse, condemnation, in her eyes.

"Now, I feel certain there's another baby. I think she's done it again. I really do."

I went on and on, unloading the burden which had threatened to crush me for so long. I told her about the bag for life that I buried Helen in. The stains on my jeans. The smell in Tom's car. And the infamous, monstrous, story of the Red Bin.

Pat didn't interrupt me once. She listened intently to each and every excruciating detail. At one point, I was shaking violently and I felt her drape a woollen shawl across my shoulders.

By the time I had finished speaking, it was 5am, and the first shafts of light streaked across the sky.

"You poor girl," Pat said gently.

She wasn't the sort of woman to cry or even give me a cuddle. But the compassion was shining out of her.

I was taken aback. It hadn't occurred to me that I was a victim in all of this. I had worried about baby Helen, about my own daughters, and Cath and Chris. I had even worried about my mother. But never about myself.

"I reported your mum to social services several times when you were growing up," Pat told me. "You had such a shocking childhood."

"It's carrying on, right through my adult years," I said bitterly. "I can't shake her off."

Pat mum looked me straight in the eye.

"Joa, you cannot carry this around for a moment longer," she said calmly. "If you really believe there might be a baby inside that bin, something needs to be done.

"Do you want to go to the police, to tell the truth? I promise you, it will be alright."

My teeth were clattering together. I was dripping with sweat. The end was coming. I felt like I was going to the electric chair.

"Do it," I said in a low voice. "Call the police. I'm ready."

"Are you sure?" Pat asked. "When I make the call, there's no going back."

I nodded. I knew that. I'd always known it. In a way, this was a relief. The wait, the purgatory, was over. The knowledge that I was finally going to the right thing was monumentally cathartic. Pat disappeared into the kitchen and came back with a bar of chocolate.

"Kettle's on, love," she smiled.

And then, she went into the hallway, to make the call which would change my life – and the lives around me – forever.

# CHAPTER 34

It was just a few moments later when she reappeared back in the living room.

"The police are coming," Pat said, completely calm.

I felt a shiver rip through me.

"Am I going to prison?" I asked shrilly. "Am I going to be locked up?"

Now it was here, staring at me, it was so hard to be brave. So hard to be good.

The police car pulled up outside before I had even finished my coffee. There were two officers, one male, one female. I took a deep breath. There was no going back, Pat was right. I was on the edge. I had to jump.

"What's gone on here, Joanne?" asked the female officer.

"My mum had a baby," I gushed. "She was keeping it in a red bin and so I buried it in Nanna Winnie's grave. Now I've found the red bin again, I'm too scared to look, but I think she's got another baby in there. I really do."

I rattled off the whole story like I was reading out a crazy shopping list.

"My mum tells a lot of lies," I finished, lamely.

The officers looked at each other and the male one knelt down, in front of me.

"Have you had a lot to drink?" he asked.

I nodded.

"I did have a few vodkas at the Ann Summers party," I admitted.

The words left my mouth before I realised how they must sound and I saw the officers exchange glances, which said: "We've a right one here!"

"I'm not drunk," I said fiercely.

The officer took a deep breath and said: "Do you suffer from any mental health problems at all? Delusion? Paranoia?"

I suppressed the urge to giggle. I could see how this looked to them. They thought I was a time-waster. A crackpot.

Hilarious; I had spent years plucking up the courage to speak to the police, and now I had actually done it, they didn't believe me!

I laughed again and turned it into a cough.

"She's in shock, and she's had no sleep," Pat said, by way of explanation. "But she's telling you the truth."

"We will have to go and talk to your mum," said the officers. "And then we'll come back. We'd like to you to remain here, in the meantime.

"Don't contact your mother or your siblings please. We will be in touch."

I nodded, but inside my stomach was suddenly churning. I was under house arrest. Virtually. And what on earth would mum tell them? It was anybody's guess. Surely, they couldn't take her seriously?

They had only been in the house for 20 minutes and as soon as they went, the room fell deathly silent. I could hear my heartbeat booming in my ears. It was horrible. Julie wiped away tears. Even Pat looked ruffled.

"I'll make us another coffee," she said, distractedly. "I'm sure we'll hear some news soon."

When the phone eventually rang, I jumped as though I'd had an electric shock.

"I see," said Pat, her voice filtering through from the hallway. "Yes, she'll be ready."

She came into the living room, that calmness, that kindness, etched on every line on her face.

"There's a police car on the way for you," she told me. "They just want to ask you a few questions, at the station."

I couldn't think of anything to say back. I couldn't even nod properly. And so, we waited in more silence. When the police car came, I got in the back seat, and I could almost sense all the curtains twitching in the street. A small, wicked, part of me wished Nanny Pat could be here to see it. The shame would have finished her off completely.

"Have they spoken to my mum yet?" I asked the officer.

"I haven't a clue!" he replied in a big, friendly voice. "I've just come on shift, and I've had beans on toast for breakfast!"

Again, I was stumped for a reply. I sat, rigid and terrified, until we arrived at the police station. We went inside, and I sat in the waiting room, next to the officer.

"Have you arrested my mum as well?" I demanded.

The officer made a few inquiries at the desk and came back to me.

"Your mum and your brother, Chris, have both been arrested," he told me. "I can't tell you anymore."

My immediate reaction was one of relief, at least Cath hadn't been arrested. Chris was living with mum and so it made sense that they would take them both. But I was worried about him.

The minutes dragged by.

"Do you think I could possibly go outside for a cigarette?" I asked in a small voice.

"Well," he said, again so jovial. "I really don't see why not. You're not under arrest. I'll have to come with you, mind."

As I stepped outside into the early morning sunshine, I checked my watch and it was almost 9am.

"My daughters will be wondering where I am!" I exclaimed.

And then, it hit me. What if I didn't see them again? What if I was locked up and sent straight to jail, for burying a baby? Do not pass Go. Do not collect £200. Go Straight To Jail. It could be months, years, before I saw the inside of my own home again.

I wanted to ask the policeman what kind of sentence I'd get for burying a baby, but I didn't want to implicate myself any further than I already had, if that was possible.

We'd only been back in the waiting room for a few minutes when a very small woman came out of a side door.

"Joanne?" she asked, holding the door open. "In here, please."

I took a seat at the other side of an interview table and prepared to run through the story, to tell her what was by now, old news. Instead, she raised her hand.

"Joanne Lee, I am arresting you on suspicion of murder," she said.

Her voice continued but I didn't hear the rest. I slid from my seat, onto my knees, and there was an anguished, searing, scream. It didn't sound like my voice. I'd heard it when John died. And I could hear it now.

"What the fuck has she told you?" I wailed.

I lay on the floor, hammering the plastic tiles, demented with shock and fury.

"Where is she?" I seethed, spit flying onto my clothes. "Let me see her!"

Nobody told me anything. I was led, bawling, into another room, where my photo was taken and my fingerprints were done. The officers took my hair bobble, my belt, and some loose change from my pocket. This was it. It was happening. My chest was so tight with panic. I felt like my sternum was going to snap.

"Where is she?" I demanded again, rabid with anger.

Next, I saw a police doctor, who said: "Who's the Prime Minister? What's 35 + 7? How many legs does a cat have?"

"What?" I snapped, irritated by such trivialities. "What?"

He cut off strands of my hair and clipped my finger-nails, too.

"For DNA," he explained. "I'm so sorry, because you do have lovely nails."

I felt like I had stumbled into a parallel universe, into someone else's life. I might just as well have fallen down the rabbit hole with Alice. On my way back past the front desk, I saw a board with a list of names, including 'Quirk.'

That had to be her. Or Chris. The name sent me into another boiling frenzy.

I was shown into a cell and the door clanged shut with a finality that resounded through my whole body. I had never been in a cell before. I looked around and recoiled. The walls were pale blue, stained with yellow and brown. There was a basic toilet, with no toilet roll. I had a narrow bed, so hard it could have been a concrete mattress. There was an all-pervading smell of urine, like the stairwell of a dodgy car-park. And the tiny window of frosted glass was made of 35 separate blocks. I counted them, over and over, to try to calm myself. My breathing was too fast. My mind was too crazy. The sensible me was trying to sort it out.

But the rest of me was furious, bubbling with a vicious, poisonous, hatred that terrified me. All my life, all my bloody life, I had picked up after her. She had leaned on me, used me, shamelessly exploited me, at every twist and turn. But nothing, nothing could have prepared me for this. It was the ultimate betrayal, the final thrust of the knife. She might just as well have stabbed me in the back and left me to bleed to death.

That night was cold and lonely. The blanket was pitifully thin and rough and I wrapped myself in the newspaper, off the floor, to try to keep warm. By the next morning, after a second night without sleep, I was so weary I was dropping, yet I was too wired to even close my eyes. An officer brought me a tiny bowl of cornflakes with warm milk and I pushed it away in disgust. I couldn't even think about eating.

The cell door opened again and the same officer asked if I wanted a solicitor.

"Yes, please," I replied dully.

I hadn't considered it until now. Stupidly, I hadn't thought I would need one. A duty solicitor came and took notes on everything I said.

And then, the CID officers came, again one male, one female.

"Tell us everything you know, Joanne," said the bloke.

I had kept the whole horrifying episode secret for so long. And now, in the space of 24 hours, I was going over it yet again. I tripped through the details, crippled with anxiety and fatigue.

"Take it slowly," said the female officer, gently.

I warmed to her. But the male officer stood over me, glowering, intimidating me. He was a big, well-built man and I wanted to ask him to back off, but I was afraid of how it might sound. I was sure it was part of their 'good cop, bad cop' routine, but it was working on me. I was alarmed by him.

Throughout the whole interview, I told two lies. The first, that Cath didn't know I had buried the baby. I didn't want her dragged into this hell. The second, I told them I had used my car, not Tom's, to bury the baby. I didn't see that it mattered. And I didn't want to implicate him either. He was nothing do with this.

Other than that, every single word I said was true.

The police gave nothing away, and afterwards, I was taken back to the cell.

And then, a second solicitor arrived.

"There was a conflict of interests with your original solicitor," he explained. "So I will represent you instead if that's OK."

He didn't elaborate. But I realised, slowly, that the first solicitor had obviously interviewed mum, too. There was the conflict. And so, she was here. She was feet away from me. I somehow felt as though I might be able to sniff her out. Smell the toxicity.

The new solicitor, Chris Bivon, was a nice chap without being over-friendly.

"I have some news for you," he said slowly. "The police searched your mum's house and they found three babies."

There was a split-second pause as it hung there.

"Three!" I screamed. "No! No! No!"

All at once, it was black then multi-coloured, hot then cold, swirling around me. I felt like I was spinning. In nothingness. Down another rabbit hole.

Snap. Back to reality.

"Three babies, it's a very serious matter indeed," said Mr Bivon.

But I was zig-zagging off on another lunatic tangent.

"Are you sure there's three?" I gasped. "How on earth could she fit three babies in that bin? Did she squash them in?

"God, she must have *crammed* them in!"

The solicitor looked rightfully appalled at my focus on the practicalities.

"I don't know," he muttered uncomfortably. "I really don't know."

I was reeling, my mind lurching back and forth, the mental equivalent of the huge pirate ships that seesaw violently back and forth at the fair.

"This a horror film," I babbled. "This is Rose West. Myra Hindley. And…" I finished on a hysterical shriek: "I'm up for murder."

The breath was abruptly sucked from me as all at once, the jigsaw pieces slotted in together. There were four dead babies. So would I be blamed for four murders? Would I be jailed for life or drowned on the ducking stool?

Every time I managed to calm myself I would suddenly be gripped by another wave of terror, and I heard myself screeching like a banshee at the solicitor.

"Three!" I yelled. "How could she? How could she?"

He promised to find out what he could, but I imagine he felt almost as out of his depth as I was. He looked shellshocked by the whole situation. He was, after all, dealing with a woman who had buried a baby with her bare hands and found three more in a red bin. If I was him, I'd have sat a little further away from me.

No sooner had he gone than the CID officers returned for round two.

"I've told you everything," I insisted.

They took me to another interview room and as we walked along the corridor, I looked straight ahead, and suddenly caught sight of mum, walking the other way, flanked by two officers.

"She's here!" I spat, venom surging through my veins.

Before I could reach her, she was pulled away, into a side room, until we had passed. Now I had confirmation she was here. So where was Chris?

"Please, tell me where he is," I pleaded. "I need to know he's safe."

But the officers were tight-lipped. Instead, I had to go through it all again. Every last word of it. I repeated the same two lies. I repeated the same desperate truths.

At the end of it, the female officer said: "When you've received your belongings, you can go home. You will be on police bail. You will have to surrender your passport."

I almost cried with gratitude. I had to sign an agreement to stay away from my mum, and then I stumbled, dazed, out into the sunshine, trying to rethread my belt around the loops in my jeans. I scanned the street, wondering wildly where the nearest phonebox might be. It was August Bank Holiday Monday 2009, and the roads were thankfully quiet.

I prayed nobody would see me. To passers-by, I looked like a disgrace – a middle-aged mess on my way home from an all-night party. My hair was a state and my face was streaked with two-day old make-up. I was so tired, I could hardly walk in a straight line. To my relief, I spotted a smashed-up call box at the far end of the street.

My hands trembling, I reversed the charges and called Cath. Natalie answered.

"Where are you, mum?" she demanded. "I'm on my way."

Within minutes, there she was, driving towards me. Julie was in the passenger seat. Seeing two friendly faces, two faces that I loved, was too much for me, and I burst into tears.

"Mum, you look like a tramp!" Natalie exclaimed. "And you smell!"

My tears turned to laughter. I hadn't had a wash, or cleaned my teeth, for two days. I was delirious with exhaustion and distress.

But I was just so glad to be going home.

# CHAPTER 35

I turned my key in the door, walked into the living room, and stopped short. For a moment, I thought we'd been burgled. And then, quickly, I realised that the police had been in. It had been ransacked. Totally ruined.

"You know what," Natalie said, surveying the scene over my shoulder. "This looks just like your mum's house! They've trashed it."

She was right. I had spent my whole adult life paying painstaking attention to cleanliness, tidiness and hygiene. So desperate was I not to be like my mother, my home was clinical. But the police search had somehow dragged me down to her level; it was as though they were putting me back in my rightful place and I hated it.

Whole drawers had been emptied onto beds and onto the floor. The washing basket had been upended onto the kitchen tiles.

All I wanted was a hot shower and a sleep in my own bed. But I had to find Chris. And I had to clean up my house. And I had to get used to the idea that I was up for murder.

Samantha, 17, was in her bedroom. But, as we polished and cleaned, she was brimming with questions.

"What's going on, mum?" she asked. "I couldn't believe it when the police arrived. I thought they were burglars at first!"

The police had told her to leave the house, and a social worker had come too. But Samantha was defiant.

"I told them I wasn't going anywhere with a social worker," she said fiercely. "I went to dad's instead."

I felt dreadful.

"You must have been so upset," I said. "I'm sorry."

Samantha smiled.

"I can stand up for myself, mum," she replied. "I was fine."

She was studying law, at college, and she was bright, as well as feisty. After the police had gone, she'd come home and seen the mess – and gone to her bedroom to wait for me.

Slowly, I put my house back together again. But there were things missing. My computer and Samantha's laptop had gone. All her college work was stored on it. Also missing was a box of keepsakes from under my bed. Inside, was a bundle of old photos, a watch which had belonged to my great grand-parents, an old collar from Nanny Edith's dog. They meant nothing to anyone else, but to me, they were so precious.

Hidden in my bedroom was a small red book, which was my diary. Inside was an account of everything I had done, starting with Helen's burial. It was a book of facts, the date of her burial, the timeline of mum's weight gain, her various boyfriends, her odd behaviours. It was my attempt to make some sense of the chaos. And I'd written down my thoughts and feelings too. When Helen would have been five years old, I realised she would – should – have been starting school. I thought about her every Christmas, and every anniversary.

I scrabbled amongst the clothes, jewellery and make-up, all scattered around the bedroom – and suddenly I spotted it, hidden under a pile of shoes. The police hadn't found it!

I grabbed it, took it downstairs, into the sink, and set it on fire. Watching it burn, I felt a strange, strangulating, sense of loss. It was, in all likelihood, the only record that Helen had ever existed. I was her link with the world. Her bridge between life and death.

But I felt it had to be destroyed. There were no lies in there. But Cath was heavily implicated. Tom's car was mentioned. I didn't want them involved.

I felt angry too. I was being made to act like a suspect. I was being forced into thinking like a criminal.

After burning the book, I went upstairs to shower and clean my teeth. And then, I set about cleaning the house again. It wasn't so much that the place was dirty. But it *felt* dirty.

With my phone in the crook of my neck, I started calling every police station in the North West, to try to find Chris. And, whilst I waited on an endless series of holds, I began scrubbing my kitchen until it shone.

Abruptly, as I was mopping the floor, a voice came on the line.

"Your brother is being held at Kirkby police station," said an officer.

"Thanks," I gasped, ripping off my rubber gloves. "I'm on my way."

As it if was meant to be, the doorbell went and I found Tom on the doorstep.

"What the hell is going on?" he asked.

"Take me to Kirkby," I replied, ushering him back up the path. "I'll tell you on the way."

"What's going on?" Tom demanded. "What the hell are you up to?"

Understandably he was full of questions but I was in no mood for it. He'd heard a rumour I'd been arrested but he didn't know why. I swatted his questions away like midges.

"Leave it, Tom," I retorted. "I'm in trouble with the police. I need to see Chris. Please, just drive."

"The police!" he gasped. "I'm not sure I should get involved. I don't know what to do."

Suddenly, I bristled.

"You don't know what to do!" I said, my voice oozing cold contempt. "How the hell do I know what to do, Tom? My life is falling to pieces around my ears. Have you thought about me? About my kids?"

My voice was rising. I had so much anger and fear, festering under the surface, and I knew it was important to snap back under control before I swung right out of it.

I clamped my mouth shut and we drove the rest of the way in a frosty silence. It was our first row. As it was, it was soon forgiven and forgotten, because I had bigger problems to address.

And the first, as we pulled up outside the police station, was Chris. I walked inside, straight up to the desk, and asked for news. But the sergeant was stony-faced.

"Is he here?" I asked. "Has he been here? I need to see him. He has seizures. He will need a doctor."

He refused to tell me anything. I had no choice but to swallow my frustration and walk back outside. As we were driving home, Cath called.

"Chris has just landed here," she said breathlessly. "He's in a state, but he's safe."

I was desperate to see him. We diverted to Cath's house and parked outside. I could hear Cath shouting and wailing even from the street.

"It's like the Moors murders!" she was screaming. "We're going to be all over the news. How many dead babies are there?"

"Cath!" I bawled, as I burst in through the front door. "Calm down and shut up! You're not helping!"

But at the sight of Chris, my voice withered and died. It had started to rain late that morning, and Chris was soaked to the skin. He was wearing shorts, a pair of work boots, and nothing else.

"They arrested me straight out of bed," he shivered. "I had no money, nothing. I've walked all the way up the East Lancs road in the pouring rain, without even a T-shirt."

It was a good hour's walk from the police station to Cath's house.

"You poor thing," I said. "I'm so sorry."

I was furious with the police. It should have been clear that Chris needed support. Yet they had let him walk home, without a penny to his name, in torrential rain.

"I tried to ask for help, but everyone I spoke to just crossed the road," he said.

I looked at him, all bedraggled and his hair plastered wet against his head, and I suddenly started to giggle.

"I'm not surprised," I laughed. "You look like you've escaped from somewhere!"

Cath started to laugh too, and soon Chris was chuckling. A good laugh was much the same as a good cry. And afterwards, we felt ready to face the world.

# CHAPTER 36

Chris told us that mum had been bailed to stay out of St Helens, and as far as we knew, she had gone to stay with her sister, Dish.

"That's a line in the sand," I said firmly. "And to think, I asked Dish for help."

Chris had arranged to go and stay with his dad, Karl. Mum's house was a crime scene, and out of bounds.

"It's like Cagney and Lacey," Cath spluttered, still spiralling. "A crime scene! Our own mother! What next?"

Late at night, back at home, I dialled dad's number with shaking hands. I was dreading this. But it had to be done.

"What's going on?" he asked immediately. "I've got a message to call Merseyside police."

And instantly, I was zapped back to being a little girl again, stepping off the edge of the kerb, with dad lecturing me on the difference between 'Right' and 'Wrong.'

CHAPTER 36

It had all seemed so clear, back then. Not so much now…

"I thought I was doing the right thing," I insisted. "I wanted dignity for the baby. I wanted a decent burial. I had no idea about the other babies, none at all."

I sucked in my breath, bracing myself for a thunderbolt. But instead, dad was calm and kind.

"What do you need me to do?" he asked. "I'm here for you."

His compassion shamed me. I felt like such a disappointment, as a daughter.

"This is not your fault," dad said gently. "We both know what your mum is like.

"I've had my own doubts about her, which I never told you.

"There was one time, years ago, when she had a bleed on the bathroom floor. I never knew what it was."

I felt myself trembling. We would probably never know. And suddenly, I was very tired. Tired by all these babies, lost souls, tortured spirits.

That night, I collapsed into bed, and despite myself, I slept. But in the early hours, I was suddenly jolted awake.

"Murder!" I shrieked, still half-asleep. "Murder!"

Every nerve in my body was jangling. I got up for a cigarette and a coffee, and wrapping my dressing gown around myself, I went to sit by the kitchen window.

We had a small, rather ordinary garden. I'd never given it much thought before. But now, as the first light of dawn broke through, I saw it for the first time in sharp focus, every flower – every weed – every broken paving stone. It was like an acid trip, I could almost hear each blade of grass growing, pushing through the earth.

"It's a beautiful garden," I said softly to myself. "I'm so lucky to live here."

I looked around the kitchen, suddenly emotional, remembering the laughs and the rows we'd had, around our dining table. But, most fondly of all, I thought back to the mundaneness of the school mornings, as the girls dallied over their breakfasts and stressed and worried over lost homework. And the bickering over Sunday lunches, Natalie refusing to finish her veg, Samantha failing to clear her plate. I stared too at the little photos, stuck to the fridge with magnets, memories now suddenly so precious, so vital.

It was nothing special. It was just an average little house. But it was special to me. It was home. My home. Yet for how much longer?

Later that morning, I got a call from one of mum's neighbours.

"I'm sorry to hear you've had some trouble," she said delicately. "Thing is, the council have been out to board up your mum's house. But they've locked one of the cats inside."

It was a shock, but I realised the house would have to be sealed off, for the police investigation.

"I'll be over shortly," I said. "Thanks for letting me know."

I buckled as I arrived outside. The doors and windows were covered with a thick green mesh. And behind, I could hear the unmistakeable sound of mum's cat, Gizmo, crying. The other two cats, Gadget and Oliver, were running around in the street.

"I've been pushing treats through the mesh," said the neighbour, coming out to greet me. "But she won't last long in there, poor thing."

I nodded and thanked her. Then I rang the council and they agreed to open the house for me. I would have to go inside. I had no choice.

I took a deep breath and waited. When the council worker finally arrived, along with a police officer, I felt spooked. I wanted to go in the house. And yet I didn't. It was a bit like watching a scary film, from behind a cushion.

As the front door opened, I took a step into the hallway – and froze. In one way, it was the same old familiar house, all mum's furniture and belongings were there. It had been ransacked, by the police, but of course mum's house was in a perpetual state of disarray so it didn't look too much worse than usual.

But there was an alien and ghoulish feel to the place. Perhaps because it was boarded up, and it was dark and gloomy. Or maybe, I thought, because the three baby spirits – the three forgotten souls – had been disturbed and were hovering, in distress, above us.

Suddenly, the cat appeared in the hallway and I jumped.

"Come on," I said, scooping her up. "Let's go home."

I adopted the three cats, and they came to live with the four cats I already owned. It seemed like the best solution. And over the next few days, I found myself driving past mum's house, drawn there, almost summoned by the spirits. It was a bit like driving past a pile-up and craning your neck to see the blood and guts on the road.

And one afternoon, I noticed there were things stuck inside the green mesh over the door. I slowed down, and realised they were flowers. There were dozens of them, poking through the tiny holes.

It was no doubt a thoughtful tribute from local people. Word was spreading and the house was becoming a kind of unholy shrine. A place where good and evil, birth and death, clashed and exploded against a backdrop of biblical judgement. But the flowers, dried up and pitifully inadequate, sent a surge of anger through me.

The babies were worth more than this. I jumped out of the car and yanked as many as I could out, onto the floor, to die.

# CHAPTER 37

Four days after I was allowed home, it was mine and Samantha's birthdays. I had baked a big chocolate cake, the night before, defiantly whisking the eggs and flour, determined to make her big day special. I was planning to buy candles on my way home.

Whatever happened, a birthday was a birthday. And she wasn't going to miss out.

That morning, I left for work, fluctuating between drowning criminal and proud mother, and still acutely aware that I hadn't told any of my bosses about my arrest.

Firstly, I hadn't a clue how to approach the subject without sounding completely and utterly barmy. I had a feeling they might escort me off the premises if they heard. And secondly, of course, I was desperate to keep an income coming in. The future was so uncertain and I wanted to save every penny I could to make sure the girls would be looked after, if the worst happened.

But, on the morning of my birthday, I was giving a lift to a colleague as usual and, as he got into the car, he whistled in amazement.

"I've just walked past your mum's house and you want to see all the fuss outside," he said. "Unbelievable."

"What do you mean?" I asked sharply, ramming on the brakes. "What?"

"Oh, there are loads of reporters outside the door," he said. "Sky news, the BBC. There are loads of photographers. Must be something going on in her street."

My heart felt like a sack of stones inside me. I could hardly hold my head up. I had to see it for myself, and so I detoured down mum's street and sure enough, there were big TV vans bumped up on the kerb, blocking the way. There was already quite a crowd gathering, kids on their way to school, nosy neighbours, one woman with her hair in curlers.

I hissed under my breath and then we drove to work in silence. That day, of all days, the big bosses were flying over from Ireland for an important meeting.

I groaned inwardly as I pictured a press pack gathering outside my office, snatching photos of all my colleagues as they nipped out on their lunch hour.

I was for it. Doomed. Facing the sack.

But I was getting used to this death-walk by now. I had done it before. I walked into work, straight into my manager's office, and gave him a quick summary of my eventful weekend.

CHAPTER 37

"I'm so sorry," I finished. "Please don't sack me. Please."

His head in his hands, he took a deep breath and said: "We'll do what we can, Joa."

It was just a simple sentence, yet it reduced me to tears. Kindness, at a time like this, was unbearable. I couldn't cope with people looking out for me, taking care of me. Maybe I wasn't used to it. Or maybe I just couldn't let my guard down. Either way, it was those little kindnesses that killed me, every time.

One manager went out to close the big red gates outside our offices. We were safe from invasion, at least. But then, the phone began to ring, relatives, friends, reporters on the sniff, Cath on the edge of a nervous breakdown. It was endless.

"Cath, stop calling me," I pleaded. "I am trying to work. I am trying to hang on to my bloody job."

"It's on the news!" she sobbed. "The TV, radio, local paper. It's everywhere."

Oh God," I breathed.

I felt like a fugitive, under siege. They were coming, ever closer. And they were after me.

At lunchtime, the big bosses arrived from Ireland. Steeling myself, I made a beeline for the MD. We had a good working relationship, I had spoken to him on the phone many times, and he beamed and held out a hand when he spotted me.

"I need a word in private," I mumbled.

Out in the corridor, I opened my mouth and the whole thing came tumbling out, like a bucket of frogs, jumping all over the place. I wasn't even sure I had it all in the right order.

"Woah," he said, raising a hand. "Slow down. I've just heard this story on the radio on my way here. Are you telling me this is you?"

I nodded. He stared hard at me, as if he didn't believe it. And I had to admit, I hardly believed myself either. I felt like I was looking in at someone else's disaster.

"We'll do what we can," he promised. "Don't worry."

Again, his support was unbearable. I was unspeakably grateful but crushed too. I'd have had dealt with it better if he'd sacked me on the spot. The whole office was wonderful, fielding calls from the press, denying they had ever heard of me. But then, Mark rang.

"I've got the girls with me," he said in a tight voice. "The police are outside your house. You need to get back now."

I swallowed and grabbed my bag. The last thing I wanted was to walk out of my job. But I had no choice.

When I pulled up outside my house, I swore quietly. There was a huge yellow police van parked in the street, and two officers at my gate.

"What the hell is going on?" I demanded. "My children are inside."

"We're here for your protection," explained an officer. "We're worried about a backlash – given the nature of the case."

I could feel the blood draining from my face, right down to my toes, no doubt leaking out onto the pavement somewhere. Was I going to become some sort of Myra

Hindley figure? I shuddered. How much more of this could I take?

"You would be safer going to stay with your father, in Devon," said the officer.

My mouth fell open. On two counts. I had no idea how he knew my dad was in Devon. The resources they were pouring into researching my life was frightening. And I was irritated by it, too. And of course, the idea itself was absurd. I had a job, two children and a home. I couldn't just run away to the seaside. This was no time for a holiday.

"I'll be absolutely fine," I clipped. "I don't need your protection, thank you. And I certainly don't need to go and stay with my dad. I'm a grown woman."

The officers refused to leave.

"We've put a marker on the house," they explained. "If you do need help, you'll be given priority."

"Bit late for that now," I muttered sarcastically.

I felt pretty sure, deep down, that most people would support me. And if they didn't, then it would be no great loss. I was used to managing on my own, after all.

I managed to calm the girls down. They were getting used to all the drama by now and as teenagers, they were expert eye-rollers. That night, I nipped out to the shop for cigarettes, and one of my next-door neighbours was walking the other way. He and I had never really spoken before. But, as he passed, he whispered: "Murderer." It was so quiet, I almost thought I'd imagined it, but I could tell, from his face, that he had said it alright.

"What did you say?" I demanded.

I was spoiling for a fight and he knew it.

"Nothing," he muttered defensively.

"Well, if you're right, you'd better watch yourself," I said wickedly. "I might come up behind you one of these nights!"

He scuttled off home like a rat and I leaned on a garden wall and giggled. It was my birthday after all – I was allowed to have some fun.

# CHAPTER 38

The next day, I had arranged to take Samantha out shopping, to buy her some birthday clothes. I was determined still to go ahead with our plans. We went off to Liverpool, not, I stressed to her, because we were hiding from anyone, but just because the shops were great.

"Ok mum," she smiled. "If you say so."

Once we arrived, I slipped on a huge pair of sunglasses.

"It's sunny," I insisted. "I'm not in disguise. Really."

Samantha laughed and we linked arms as we shopped. Walking along, in the sunshine, weighed down by bags of clothes and make-up for her, I felt a million miles away from all my troubles. I could almost pretend I was just a normal mum with a normal daughter on a normal birthday trip.

But then, Julie called me.

"Have you seen the Liverpool Echo?" she asked. "You're front page."

My stomach flipped. There was a newspaper stand, just yards away, and as I read the billboard, I stiffened.

'Three babies found in St Helens house. Arrests for Murder.'

I took my place in the queue, head bowed and bought a newspaper. And there, staring out from the front page, was a photograph of me and Chris. It had been taken in Florida, on holiday.

"Where on earth did, they get these photos?" I gulped.

"Facebook, probably," said Samantha, peering over my shoulder. "Funny thing is, you have sunglasses on there too, so everyone will recognise you anyway! Your disguise is useless!"

I gave her a playful slap and we bundled the newspaper into a bag.

"This is your birthday treat and we're not going to spoil it," I vowed. "Come on, let's get an ice-cream."

We sat by the waterfront, eating our ice-creams, and I tried to relax, for Samantha's sake. But inside, I was churned up. Discreetly, I pulled my hair further forward to hide my face. I kept my head down. I was terrified of someone recognising me. Of course nobody did. Nobody even gave me a second glance.

As we finished our ice-creams my phone rang again and it was Cath.

"You're on the news again!" she shrieked.

"Well, turn the bloody telly off," I snorted. "We've enough to worry about, without the press."

I was being braver than I felt. But then, hadn't that always been the way? That night, I flicked on the regional news, and there I was again. I listened, stiff, as the report claimed the gravediggers at the funeral of Ellie's baby had in fact found Helen's remains after all. They had dug up the canvas bag and, believing it contained the bones of a family pet, replaced it without reporting it.

It was only now – after the police investigation – that they had come forward.

"Well nobody bothered to tell me," I huffed. "Good job I'm on the news after all. It's my only source of information."

But the thought of Helen's body being disturbed and thrown back into the earth, like a decomposing dog, was disturbing. There was something so sordid and desperate about her burial, and I couldn't shake it.

"I'm sorry, Helen," I whispered softly. "I really am."

Though I wasn't religious, I said a little prayer for her. Then, I went for a long bath, and I felt as though I was trying to wash away more than the day's dust and dirt. Before I got into bed, I turned off my bedroom light and peered out through the window. The police van was still outside, and it whirred loudly, like a broken air-con unit. The street was literally swarming with people, walking past, waiting around, sitting in cars. Some were no doubt reporters. But most were just plain, old-fashioned nosey-parkers, wandering casually past my house, hoping for a snippet of scandal.

Funny, I had spent my whole childhood wishing someone would listen – that someone would get involved in our lives. Now the whole bloody world was here. And I just wanted them all to go away.

# CHAPTER 39

The police van stayed for three days before eventually moving on, no doubt to a more important case, and I was thrilled. If nothing else, I could get some sleep without the constant noise.

"Peace," I said. "At last."

And at the end of that week, Natalie asked, cautiously, if she could go to visit my mum. I had known this was coming. Natalie and I my mum were quite close, in their own way.

Besides, she wasn't just my mum. She was my daughters' grandmother, though they had always referred to her simply as "Bernie."

But I had no right to stop Natalie seeing her.

"Of course," I replied, heaving my own feelings aside for a moment. "Be sure not to talk about what's happened, because of the court case."

I was on edge the whole time Natalie was out. And when she returned, I flew to the door. Despite myself, I wanted information. But I wasn't sure whether I wanted my mother to be bearing up well, or to be burned at the stake.

"They didn't let me in at first," Natalie explained. "I had to knock on the door for ages and then I shouted through the letterbox.

"When they realised it was just me, Dish let me in."

She had seen my mum, and unsurprisingly, she had seemed to be her normal self.

"She didn't seem at all worried," Natalie said. "It was odd. Dish was really stressed but Bernie was fine. Her usual self, you know."

Oh yes, I knew alright. It was just what I would have expected. It would take more than a skeleton or three in the cupboard to upset her.

# CHAPTER 40

In the months that followed, my own cats, Pud, Tiffany, Fudge and Velcro, all died, one by one. Pud simply vanished and never came back. Tiffany had kidney failure and had to be put to sleep at the vets. Poor Velcro had a stroke, and Fudge simply died, quite inexplicably, in my arms.

Mum's three cats, who I'd adopted after her arrest, ran around the house, perfectly healthy.

"It's the Middlehurst curse," I said with a hollow laugh. "She's killing my cats off."

It was ridiculous. But I was almost starting to believe it.

And whilst I was busy mourning and burying my pets, and cursing the curse, I had various different police officers, calling at the house, asking me questions. We went round in circles until I was sick of the sound of my own voice.

"Is she trying to say these babies were mine?" I asked. "What's she telling you?"

They didn't say. They didn't give anything away. So I soldiered on, telling the truth every time, desperately hoping that they would believe me.

Privately, I resented them swarming in and out of my house, just as they pleased. But I knew I had no choice. One day, unannounced, a social worker called round.

"You can't look after your granddaughter unsupervised," she said sternly. "Or any other children for that matter."

I felt myself shrivel inside.

"I look after my granddaughter every weekend," I snapped. "And I baby-sit my sister's kids, too. I'm not prepared to stop. I'm doing nothing wrong."

She opened her mouth to protest and I said calmly: "I want you to get out please."

She picked up her bag and left and my face stung with bitter tears. The humiliation was hard to take. My whole life was falling apart.

Every Saturday night, Natalie's 2-year-old daughter, Kiera came to me for a sleepover. And I would often baby-sit Cath's youngest, Aaron, too. It seemed unbelievably cruel to stop them coming to stay.

Cath had the same visit from social services and gave them the same, angry response. But I realised our defiance was putting Kiera and Aaron in danger.

"Just agree to everything," I told her wearily. "As soon as this is over, we can go back to how it was."

Increasingly, I just didn't have the fight in me any more.

Christmas came and went and I cooked a big dinner for the whole family. I remembered the Christmas celebrations Nanny Pat had organised. Posh china on top of the table, blood-curdling revelations lurking beneath. Those family secrets were like rats running under the floorboards.

All I could think, as everyone chatted and clinked glasses around me, was that this could be my last Christmas as a free woman for a very long time indeed.

It would be March 2010 – seven agonising months after my arrest – that the yoke was lifted from my shoulders. My liaison officer, Mike Bevan, called round to see me one evening after I had finished work.

"What do you want this time?" I asked wearily. "I've told you everything. Everything."

I felt like I was doing circuits on a hamster wheel. The same questions. The same answers. It was physically draining.

"I've come to tell you there will be no further action against you," he said, with a smile.

I took a moment to drink it in.

"No charges?" I asked quietly. "Nothing?"

"That's right," he replied.

"And what about Chris?" I asked.

"Same for Chris," Mike replied. "But your mother will face charges."

Suddenly weak and wobbly, I sank to the couch and the tears flowed. I realised, minutes later, that Mike was still waiting patiently, and I jumped to my feet, suddenly filled with energy.

"I can tell you about the case now," he said. "But where to start?"

He explained that forensics had done months of tests on all four babies. One had been found in the red bin. Two were discovered in a canvas bag, by the side of her bed.

I groaned with a strange mixture of disgust and embarrassment. Even now, she had the ability to turn my stomach. Most women her age kept their knitting in a bedside bag. Not my mum. She had babies' bodies.

In a funny way, I felt a sense of relief that all three babies had not been squashed into the red bin. I had been haunted by gruesome images, night after night, of their tiny bodies, broken and bruised, crammed into the confines of the bin.

"All were full-term," Mike told me. "All, according to your mother, were stillborn. We can't prove otherwise. We can't prove anything else.

"Two had broken ribs, one had an injury to a cheek-bone."

I recoiled in horror. I had believed – hoped – that the babies had been premature. That they had not stood a chance. But this was not the case.

"They were all girls," Mike added. "Four daughters."

For some reason, the revelation sent another chill down my spine. Four little girls. Four pure, white souls. Damned by the Middlehurst witches.

Mum, Mike explained, had named them Sheila, Ann and, of course, Helen. There was no name for the poor baby in the red bin.

"Your mum said that Sheila and Ann were twins," Mike continued. "We can't prove or disprove that. It's possible, though very rare, to have twins with two different fathers. That's what she says happened to her. We have to take her word for it."

I rolled my eyes. I pitied the officers working on her case. They were dealing with a consummate and compulsive liar.

As the investigation progressed, I learned more and more. Mike told me the babies were born roughly between 1986 and 1997. Their bodies had been so badly decomposed that the officer who discovered them had been badly affected.

"Can you think of who the fathers might be – using those dates?" Mike asked.

My head was spinning. Those years had been chaotic. I thought back to the blood-stained carpet, mum's yo-yo weight gain, the years and years of deceit. Mark's name flashed in my head in block capitals and neon lights. But I tried to stay calm. Biting on my pen, I scribbled a short list and handed it to Mike.

"Thanks Joanne," he said. "This will be a big help."

After he left, I could think of nothing else. I called Cath and we came up with a thousand more theories. The next time Mike called, I was desperate for information.

"Who were the babies' fathers?" I pressed. "Did you find out? I need to know."

But Mike sighed apologetically.

"That's confidential," he replied. "I'm sorry. But I can tell you that your mother is going to be charged with concealing the births, and nothing more."

I wasn't exactly surprised. But I was angry. I felt she was getting away lightly. Part of me was still smarting over my own arrest, and I wanted to see her locked up for life. And yet, in calmer moments, I knew she needed help, not punishment. I blamed her upbringing and her family, as much as her.

But this way, we would never really know the truth of what happened to those four, innocent little girls.

I, more than anyone else, knew what mum was capable of. And these charges merely skimmed the surface of her rancid birthing pool.

# CHAPTER 41

One afternoon soon after, Cath called me, bubbling with news.

"Dad just rang me," she said. "You won't believe this, Joa. He is the father of one of the babies."

I was in shock. I had never considered that Karl might be one of the fathers. I had imagined that the babies were born after mum and Karl had separated, after her life fell well and truly off the rails.

"Dad is really upset," Cath said. "It's hit him badly."

I felt for Karl. If he'd known mum was carrying his baby, he'd have been supportive. He'd have looked after them both. He'd always been a good dad and stepdad, a decent man. It made the whole sorry, seedy episode seem yet more tragic.

And that night, Natalie was waiting for me, sitting at the kitchen table, her head in her hands.

"Dad is father to one of the babies," she croaked. "I can't believe it. I can't believe he could do that."

Her face was tear-stained and she trembled as she spoke. For me, it was no shock. More a dull sort of confirmation that this was slightly worse than the worst I had feared all along.

The police had been to see Mark and he had, in turn, confided in Natalie.

"I'm sorry I never believed you, mum," she said softly.

"You're not the one who should be apologising," I replied.

Funny though, those who ought to have been apologising had nothing at all to say. I didn't hear from Mark. Or mum.

We heard, through friends of Cath, that the third father was a man who'd had a brief relationship with mum.

Armed with information, I called Mike.

"Me and Cath know who the babies' fathers are," I told him. "And we would like to give them a proper burial. Please."

It had played on my mind, itched like a scab, knowing the babies had not been laid to rest. As with Helen, I wanted them to have dignity.

"Of course, we'd like to invite all the babies' fathers," I offered. "And my mother, I suppose."

I couldn't work out which would be more bizarre – if she did or did not attend. They were, after all, her babies. Her four children. And yet.

We would have to wait, we were told, for the babies' bodies to be released by the coroner. But after that, there was no reason why we couldn't organise a funeral.

# CHAPTER 42

In July 2010, mum appeared for the first time at Liverpool Crown Court, charged with concealment of birth. I went along, too wise and too weary to expect any kind of remorse. But I wanted to see her, all the same. And I wanted her to see me, too.

In a hearing lasting just a couple of minutes, she was formally charged, and then she disappeared, without even speaking. It was something of an anti-climax and I looked at Cath, who was with me, and sighed. Like anything involving our mother, this was not going to be straightforward.

Two months on, she made a second appearance, and this time admitted the charge. Cath and I were in the public gallery once again, waiting for the next shameful instalment of our family life to be played out in public.

"We could have our own family soap opera," Cath whispered in my ear.

"You're joking," I retorted. "Nobody would watch it. They'd all say it was too far-fetched for real life. It's totally unrealistic."

A barrister began to speak and a hush descended upon the court room. Even though it wasn't me in the dock, I still felt like jelly. It was a daunting place.

He explained that police believed mum had given birth at various times between 1986 and 1997 but none of the babies had been registered. She had never even told her GP she was pregnant.

After her marriage had ended, the court heard she had started drinking heavily and had casual sexual encounters.

DCI Neil Bickley, of Merseyside police, said: "Forensic investigations tell us Bernadette Quirk was the mother of all the babies, although in interview she only accepted being the mother of twins found in her home and the baby at the cemetery. She did not acknowledge being the mother of the fourth child.

"There were three separate fathers who we managed to trace and speak to during the investigation. None knew Quirk had fallen pregnant."

Experts in child mortality, pathology and genetics were brought in from all over the country to advise the inquiry team and give their opinions.

Police said "all potential charges" were considered – including murder.

But a doctor at Cardiff university found "no independent signs of life" while Professor Jim Neilson, from Liverpool university and Liverpool women's hospital, said while it was "unusual" for four babies to be stillborn at full term, Quirk's "chaotic" lifestyle could have impacted on prenatal health.

DCI Bickley said: "People have now said to us they did notice there were times where she seemed to lose weight all of a sudden.

"This was a very different investigation, made particularly difficult because of the condition of the babies. They were just skeletal remains.

"We just had to keep on interviewing people who pointed us in the direction of others and soon we were able to put together a picture of what we believe happened.

"Bernadette Quirk kept this secret with her. She did not come to us, we went to her, and she certainly was not telling us willingly.

"Now the family are keen to give these babies a proper, private burial."

Hearing our darkest, most delicate, secrets, discussed in a public court – was mortifying. I felt humiliated. The court heard the facts and only the facts. I had buried a baby, I had discovered three more, I had lived a life of squalor and chaos with my depraved mother. It sounded so cold. So damning. I wanted to stand up and tell them how, on every anniversary, I had thought of little Helen and my heart had wept as I imagined her taking her first steps, lisping her first words, skipping off to her first day at school. I was desperate to tell the courts – to tell whoever would listen – that I had cared. I had cried. I had agonised over this. And I would do so for the rest of my life.

I didn't recognise myself, the way the barrister spoke about me. And I wanted no part of it all. I wanted to shake mum off and leave her in the gutter. Yet we were bound together. Shackled by these skeletons. And nothing could ever change that.

# CHAPTER 43

In mid-November 2010, I realised my period was late. But I dismissed it, believing it was just stress. Then, I started to feel queasy. With a sinking feeling, I bought a pregnancy test. When it was positive, I covered my face and wept.

I was fond of Tom though our relationship had taken a backwards step since my arrest. And the timing, with mum's court case approaching, was not good.

Irrationally, I cursed my mother for the pregnancy. I felt sure, with a sixth sense, that she had damned me. It was the Middlehurst curse again.

The reasonable part of me reminded me I'd obviously forgotten to take my contraception, at some point. But even then, I managed to land it on my mum.

"This would never have happened, if it wasn't for all the stress," I said.

Even so, when I calmed down, I was clear about the future. I was having a baby, and I would love and cherish it, just as I had my other children.

Somehow, somehow, I would cope.

That night, I confided in Natalie, and she wrapped her arms around me.

"Aw mum," she said softly. "What are you going to do?"

Mum was due in court to be sentenced the following week, in December 2010. So I decided to get that over with, before I told everyone my news.

I wanted to see what she had to say.

Chris, Cath, their dad, Karl, and Natalie all came along too. We got the train to Liverpool and seated ourselves neatly in the public gallery at Liverpool Crown Court. It was nerve-racking, staring at the dock and imagining myself standing there.

"This could have been you," I told myself.

Mum was led into court and I glared at her, but she made no eye contact. Strangely, she was wearing a blonde wig, and leaning heavily on a walking stick. One for disguise. One for sympathy. I was cynical, but who could blame me? As she raised her head, I saw tears trickling down her cheeks. Then, she mumbled something about an apology to her family, and I bristled.

"She's at it again," I seethed. "More lies. More games."

There was an exchange between solicitors, and then a judge informed mum that she would be given a two-year supervision order, under strict supervision.

"Well, good luck with that," I whispered to Cath. "Anyone trying to supervise her will have a job on their hands."

Despite everything, I was relieved she hadn't been jailed. Prison was not the right place for a woman like her and I wasn't sure she could have coped with it. She needed help, treatment, education and guidance. That said, she was walking away – albeit on a stick – from a bin full of death.

As I stood up to leave the courtroom, I suddenly felt a wet, sticky feeling between my legs.

"Natalie," I whispered. "I need to get to a bathroom."

I felt sick as I stumbled into the ladies' loos. And, as I locked the cubicle, my worst fears were confirmed.

"I think I'm having a miscarriage," I said to Natalie. "I need to get to hospital."

We went straight to the nearest A and E. And a scan revealed that there was no heartbeat.

"So sorry," said the nurse, as she switched off the monitor and wiped down the trolley for the next patient. "So sorry."

I was booked in to have the foetus removed three days later. I felt far away, disconnected and empty. Achingly empty.

That night curled up in bed and still bleeding, the memories of John's birth came rushing back. I was flooded with guilt and self-blame. I hadn't wanted this baby, not at first. It stuck in my throat to admit it. But there it was.

And now, just days later, it was dead. Dead on the day of the court case. Dead like all the other babies. Was this my punishment? Another life snuffed out. How many more? I felt like mum was a jinx on all new life.

"You can always try again," Natalie told me. "If you really want another baby, you should go for it, mum."

I did want another baby, deep down. I realised that now. But I couldn't shake a nagging doubt that perhaps I would never be able to have another baby. It would never be *allowed*. The Middlehurst curse was hanging around my neck like a rusty chain.

# CHAPTER 44

If I had thought the media frenzy around the court case would die down now, I was wrong. Cath, Chris and I were harassed by journalists and paparazzi.

They parked in the street outside and ambushed me as I left the house.

"We want your side of the story," they urged. "Tell us what really happened. This is your chance."

They even managed to sniff out where Natalie lived too. She came out of her front door one morning to find a reporter from the Daily Mirror waiting on her path.

"Do you know where we can find Bernadette's Quirk's family?" he asked.

"Not a clue," Natalie replied glibly. "Never heard of her."

I got dozens of letters through the post, all asking me to speak out.

"Nosey little bleeders," I said. "Have they nothing better to do?"

Cath got the same letters, too. But whereas I was open and blunt about what had happened, she was upset and worried by all the attention.

I don't want people to find out she's my mum," Cath fretted. "I'm worried about losing my job."

"Just ignore the letters," I advised, ripping them all up and throwing them away. "Forget about the press."

But as the days went by, I began to change my mind. I thought more and more about Helen and my sisters.

One day, I got a sympathy card from an old friend pushed through my front door. It was addressed to our family and, as I read it, I saw red. It seemed deeply inappropriate. Like the flowers pushed through the grills on mum's old house.

I realised people were actually feeling sorry for us – and for mum, too.

Because mum had pleaded guilty in court, the facts of the case had never been heard. People were making their own minds up instead.

Another day, a family friend stopped me in the street and gave me a sympathetic smile.

"How's your mum doing?" she asked gently. "I was so sorry to hear of her loss. So sorry."

I stared at her. My jaw worked up and down but I couldn't find the words. Apoplectic with silent rage, I just walked away. I didn't know where to start.

It had never occurred to me that people might actually feel sympathetic towards mum. Did they think she had been the victim of some terrible accident? That she had been mis-represented and misunderstood by the courts?

And it got worse. Cath called round one day, her face a mixture of upset and annoyance.

"You'll never believe this," she said. "I overheard people talking about mum at work – but they thought the babies belonged to you! They think mum took the rap for you! I set them straight, but I could see they weren't convinced."

It wasn't entirely unexpected. This was something I had worried about myself, especially during the police investigation. But it still stung.

"Well, people will say there's no smoke without fire," I replied eventually. "I was arrested for murder, after all. I was the one who buried the baby.

"I can understand why strangers would think I had something to do with it all. I'm the right age, too, for babies.

"There's nothing we can do, Cath. We just have to let people talk. Those that know us have stood by us and that's all we can ask."

Nobody ever said anything directly to my face, but the rumours were there. It was all second- and third-hand gossip, passed around the community before finding its way back to me.

Sometimes, I wasn't sure what was worse, the allegation that the babies were mine, or the idea that mum would actually cover and lie for me. The very idea that mum would put herself out in any way for her children was as ludicrous as it was abhorrent. The irony of it was devastating.

She had walked away from the mess she had created, as she always did. She had left someone else to clean up after her, because that was what she was used to.

She needed help, yes. But not sympathy. No flowers, no cards, no tender words.

She had fallen woefully short as a mother, with all of her children, dead and alive.

It was time to set people straight.

"You know what, I think we should give an interview after all," I said to Cath. "There are so many silly stories going round. Nobody has any idea of the truth of what went on – and that includes mum.

"We ought to put the facts out there, for the sake of the babies. We are their only hope."

I didn't really fancy the idea of having a cosy chat and slice of cake with the reporters and photographers who had followed me round like a bad smell for so long. But my four sisters had no voice. And this was their chance to be heard.

Cath agreed and we decided to speak together. First we read through the letters we'd received, then we made our choices. We gave the interviews, at my house, paying painstaking attention to detail.

"It feels good to get it all off my chest," Cath said afterwards.

The following week, our story went all over the world. On my way home from work, I nipped into the newsagents and grabbed a load of daily papers.

It was odd to see me and Cath, staring out from the pages, alongside lurid headlines about our mother.

Later that night, Cath called me. By now, she was working shifts as a carer.

"I went into work earlier and my patient was reading our story in the newspaper," she said. "I didn't know where to look. She was telling me all about it and didn't even realise it was me in the story!"

The following day, Kiera, my little granddaughter, found one of the newspapers on the back seat of the car, and squealed when she spotted my photo.

"Are you famous Mum-Pie?" she asked in excitement.

"Not quite darling," I smiled, quickly taking the paper from her and folding it into my bag. "I'm more infamous unfortunately. When you're older, I'll tell you all about it."

After the newspapers, came an invite to appear on This Morning TV, with Phil Schofield and Clare Rayner. Cath wasn't sure about going on telly, because she was worried about the impact on her job. She was so stressed and I didn't want to make it worse. And so, Natalie agreed to come with me instead.

We got a late train down to London and then we were taken to a hotel overnight. Natalie bounced on the bed whilst I helped myself to cheese and biscuits and a cup of tea.

"It's like being on holiday," Natalie whooped.

It was an odd feeling. We were here to talk about the 'Babies in the Bin'. And yet, here we were, giggling and enjoying all the freebies.

I couldn't help feeling somehow disrespectful and disloyal. As though I was betraying the memory of my sisters somehow.

And yet I was doing nothing wrong.

Early the following morning, a taxi came to pick us up and take us to the TV studios. Natalie and I dashed out of the hotel, still half-asleep, and it wasn't until we were in the taxi that I realised I was wearing odd boots.

"I've got your boot on!" I shrieked.

"Don't worry, I've got yours on," Natalie laughed. "We just need to swap."

When we arrived, we were taken through make-up and wardrobe, and I began to feel nervous. Clare Rayner came to meet us and kindly took my hands.

"Just be yourself, Joanne," she said. "You'll be fine."

But then, a producer came to speak to us and ran through a check-list.

"We will be live on air," he told us. "So we can't make any allegations about your mum. You can't share your views about what you think happened to those babies."

I pursed my lips. We would see about that. My whole reason for doing this was not fame, fortune or fun. I wanted to speak out for my sisters. And this was my one chance.

Under the hot lights in the studio, with Phil Schofield on the opposite couch, I suddenly felt at ease. I knew what I had to do.

"We must stress that there is no evidence the babies were harmed in any way," he said. "There is no evidence they were alive at birth."

"And there is also no evidence that they were stillborn," I interrupted loudly.

There was an awkward silence and one of the producers gave me daggers from behind the screens. I could taste the tension in the studio.

But that was that. I had made my point.

# CHAPTER 45

On a cold January morning, in a biting chill, our four half-sisters were buried at last. Co-op funerals had refused to take payment from us.

"Four babies?" asked the undertaker. "I'm so sorry for your loss, we'll do the funeral for free."

Cath and I carried out what remained of the organising. Cath had invited Karl and we knew, of course, that he would attend. Natalie had asked Mark, but he didn't come. Cath also invited the third father, because she knew him, and he accepted.

And Chris had asked mum to come, too. She had refused, as we knew she would. And yet our hearts sank with the confirmation we had never wanted – that she didn't care a jot. It stuck in my throat. But it probably would have been the same if she had come.

There were two white coffins, each pitifully small, each containing the remains of two babies.

We had asked each father to name their baby. Helen's father was not Mark as I had always suspected. We changed her name to Angelica Helen. Mark named his daughter Katie, with the middle name, Anne, which mum had chosen. And Karl's baby was called Angela Sheila. The fourth baby, possibly but not certainly a twin, was named by Cath. She'd had three sons, and had always wanted a little girl, and so it seemed appropriate for her to choose a name.

Cath decided on Elizabeth Julia. Julia was my mum's middle name. It might have seemed a little odd, twisted even, to name the baby after a mother whose bond with her children stretched no further than the umbilical cord. But instinctively, Cath and I felt it was the right thing to do. It was almost as if the name was already decided, sitting there, in our subconscious, waiting to be confirmed. She was their mother. Our mother. And try as we might, we couldn't change that.

Cath, Chris and I were all there at St Helen's crematorium together. I gave a short reading, which I had written myself.

"This shouldn't be a sad day," I insisted. "Our four sisters are at peace. They are now free."

I apologised to Helen, because of the role I had played. This was my chance to right the wrong. To redeem myself. And I alluded, too, to what I thought had happened to the babies. I did not, could not, accept that all four babies, born full-term, were born dead.

"I know the truth," I said simply.

Mum wasn't there to hear it. But I wanted to say it out loud, all the same. For me, there was a sense of relief.

But the babies' fathers were red-eyed and sombre. It was unspeakably sad for them both.

Afterwards, the ashes were scattered by the undertaker, with nobody else present. If there could be an end to this nightmare, then this was it.

# CHAPTER 46

In August 2011, I fell pregnant again. This time, I told Tom immediately, and we were both overjoyed.

"It's meant to be," he beamed.

Three weeks on, it was my 40th birthday, and I woke early filled with excitement. But, as I shifted a little in bed, I felt that same sticky sensation, and I had that same, sickly feeling of dread. Tom drove me to hospital and we waited, anxiously, for a scan.

"I'm so sorry, there's no heartbeat," said a doctor.

We drove home in a silence which was raw and heavy with grief.

In the months after the court case, Samantha left home to study criminology at university. One evening, she called home and said: "Mum, you won't believe this. The lecturer used Bernie's court case as an example in our law lecture today. I could have died of shame, there and then! Everyone was talking about her."

I felt for her. It seemed we would never, ever escape this ghoulish legacy, no matter how hard we tried.

Another time, Natalie went to a party at a house which backed onto mum's old house. As she chatted with friends, she overheard a woman loudly telling all the other guests how mum had hidden dozens of babies in her attic.

"I butted in to tell her she was exaggerating a bit," Natalie told me later. "The poor woman was mortified. I think she thought I was annoyed. But I just laughed.

"I told her we're used to tall tales in our family."

The rumours and the gossip didn't stop there. My friend, Carol, called round one day to tell me she'd heard two shoppers discussing how mum gave birth to babies and the rest of the family ate them.

"She was telling everyone that your Chris is a cannibal!" Carol spluttered. "I set her straight. Don't worry about that, Joanne."

I smiled. Truth was, these stories didn't upset me terribly. We had done our best to get the truth across in our interviews, and if people didn't want to hear it, that was their decision. The way I saw it, the reality was much worse than most of the lies anyway. Most people locally knew me and Cath and they had been kind and supportive. The others, well, mum had given them good enough reason to talk about her. So she could hardly complain when they did.

Natalie continued her occasional visits to mum. And whilst I was curious and eager for news, I didn't resent her for going. Every time Natalie came home, she'd sit at the kitchen table and smile, ready for my grilling. But it was always something of an anti-climax.

"She won't talk about the babies," Natalie said. "And if I mention anything at all connected with the court case, she just clams up. I know she won't talk about it. I'm a bit scared to bring it up with her, to be honest."

That was typical of mum. She'd chat happily about the TV schedule or the weather forecast. But scratch beneath the surface, mention something that really mattered, and she'd lash out and spit like a feral cat.

Natalie went off to visit mum one day in December 2011, and this time, she returned with an odd development.

"She has changed her name from Bernadette to Julia," she said. "All her Christmas cards from her relatives were written to Julia."

I rolled my eyes. This was mum's way of sweeping it all under the carpet, she was using her middle name to distance herself from the court case.

"Don't embarrass the family, don't upset the neighbours, whatever you do." I could almost hear Nanny Pat's voice and see her finger waggling in my face.

The irony was, of course, that we had named one of the babies Julia. And so, in a way, mum was running towards them, not further away.

That same Christmas, a parcel arrived through the letterbox. I knew, instantly, from the handwriting, that it was from mum.

I dropped it onto the table in disgust. I felt like someone had sent me a severed head in the post. Crackling with revulsion, I scribbled her address on the package and marched straight out to the postbox to send it back to her.

Later that day, Cath called.

"I got a present from mum in the post," she told me.

"You too!" I exclaimed.

Cath had opened hers. She had a Baileys gift set and some money, which we decided must be from the sale of our grandfather's home.

"More mind games," I said caustically.

I didn't for a moment think she was softening. Most probably, she needed us for something.

Even so, after Christmas, Cath decided to visit mum.

"Maybe she's changed, Joa," she said wishfully. "Maybe now, after the court case and the funerals. Perhaps this is her chance to start again, her chance to be honest with us."

"I doubt it," I sniffed.

After the visit, Cath came straight round to see me. Her shoulder sagged and she was crestfallen. Beaten.

"She's no different," she said sadly. "She's not sorry. She's not even sad. She was full of the usual lies. I'm never going again. It was a mistake."

# CHAPTER 47

The deaths of my four half-sisters were never far from my mind. And my grief seemed to lead, with crazy logic, to an overwhelming desire for another baby myself.

Tom and I were happy enough, though still living separately. My daughters were grown up with lives of their own. And I felt, at 41, that this was my last chance.

In January 2012, my period was late, and the familiar backache and nausea around coffee and booze could mean only one thing. That night, when Tom called round, I passed him a positive pregnancy stick and smiled nervously.

"Let's take it one day at a time," he said.

We were both anxious. And taking into account my two miscarriages, my GP prescribed a blood thinner, which I injected daily into my stomach. When I reached my three-month scan without any problems, we began to dare to hope.

And by 20 weeks, when the scan showed our baby was healthy, we could finally celebrate. This was a reality. We whooped with joy. We had decided not to find out the sex, although I was desperate for a son, of course it really didn't matter.

Part of me wondered whether my successful pregnancy was linked to the burial of the babies. Was this my reward, for laying them to rest? It was an odd train of thought. But one I couldn't quite shake off.

One night, in September 2012, my waters suddenly gushed, and I called Tom to take me to hospital. But my labour was very slow. All through the next day – and night – Tom paced the delivery room while I wailed in agony.

At 6.25am, on September 11, I gave birth to the most beautiful creature I had ever seen – a little boy named Alex. I wept tears of celebration, gratitude and relief. Weighing 6lbs 13ozs, he was perfect.

"I have waited 25 years to see your face," I told him gently. "For you have the same face as your big brother, John."

As I cradled him, I felt like I was standing on the top of the world. That night, with Alex sleeping peacefully beside me, I watched an anniversary programme about the 9/11 attack in America. And the stark contrast, between such hideous suffering and my boundless joy, was not lost on me. And again, I cried tears of thanks.

Maybe, just maybe, there were four little souls, four perfect white witches, looking after us from heaven.

The following day, before we left hospital, Alex had a routine hearing test. The audiologist smiled and said: "He has failed the test, but don't worry, we'll repeat it tomorrow."

I was not concerned. Nothing could have dented my happiness. The roof could fall in. I could lose my job. I could have the car, the house, hell, my whole shoe collection, repossessed– and it would not matter a jot. Because my little man was a rare prince. His arrival had brought luck, joy and endless, endless, love.

The results of the test, the following day, were the same. So we were given an audiology appointment and I was sent home.

With a new baby to think of, Tom and I decided to make our little family official, and we moved in together. My daughters had their own lives to lead now and my priority had to be Alex, especially since we suspected he might have a hearing issue.

And even in those first few weeks, I knew. Alex would squirm and cry every time I put a hat over his ears. He hated being in his Moses basket, but he was fine in his cot, with space between the bars, to look out. He would cry whenever I strapped him into his rear-facing car seat. Yet when I bought a front-facing seat instead, he was happy.

"He doesn't like anything which blocks his vision," I explained to Tom. "He's relying on his eyes, because his ears don't work. "I think he's deaf."

Tom stared at me, his jaw slack with shock. But for me, it was something I could easily cope with. And I felt certain Alex would cope too. After my years growing up with my grandparents, I felt in tune with deafness. I almost felt I could *hear* Alex's deafness.

The audiology appointment, six weeks later, confirmed it. Alex was profoundly deaf.

"My grandparents were both profoundly deaf," I explained to the audiologist.

It was thought there must be a genetic link, and Alex was referred for more tests. When I went back, for the results, the consultant greeted me with some amazement.

"I've never seen this before," he admitted. "There are actually two, totally separate, reasons for Alex's deafness."

He explained that Alex had a genetic mutation which caused deafness, as we had suspected. But he also had a physical abnormality in the bones in his ear, which caused deafness.

"Your son was meant to be deaf," said the consultant.

Unexpectedly, I found myself beaming.

"Of course he was," I replied. "He's a gift from my Nanny Edith."

It was explained that he wasn't suitable for a cochlear implant or any other type of surgery.

"But that's good, really, isn't it?" I said. "At least we know what we're dealing with."

And, if I was honest, I wouldn't have been too keen on Alex having surgery. I wasn't sure it was the right approach to 'correct' or 'cure' his deafness.

"Our son has a right to be who he is," I said. "He's part of the deaf culture, the deaf community."

Adjusting to looking after a deaf baby was not a problem for me. I hardly even saw Alex's deafness as a disability. But I noticed friends, and some relatives, were devastated on my behalf.

"So sorry," they said. "How awful. How cruel."

"Why?" I questioned. "What's the big issue?"

And it was only then, in a moment of painful clarity, that I realised how thoughtless I was being. I had grown up with deafness, I could sign. In fact, I was as happy with signing as I was with speaking.

Deafness did not scare me one bit.

But for others, and for other parents especially, this would undoubtably be traumatic.

It got me thinking. I was lucky, but there were families out there who needed support. I began asking around, through our GP surgery and the National Deaf Children's Society.

To my disappointment, there was very little on offer for families.

I knew that, more than anything, a child like Alex needed my time. The two girls, when they were small, had been my main focus. But Alex, with his extra needs, became my only focus. From the moment of his diagnosis I signed everything to him. By the time he was four months old, he could already understand simple sign language.

"Beautiful boy," I signed. "Mummy's beautiful boy."

He gurgled with laughter and I knew the message was getting through.

Every morning, as I bathed and dressed him, I would sing and sign: "You Are My Sunshine" to him. I took him for lots of walks through our local parks too, and I signed everything that we saw.

"Tree, Dog, Path, Sun," I told him.

I bombarded him with information, and he soaked it all up, like a hungry little sponge. One day, I was walking through the local park, carrying Alex, and an aeroplane zoomed overhead.

Alex looked up, squealed with delight and signed: "Aeroplane!"

It was his first word. I screamed in excitement, spinning him round in the park, whooping and crying.

From there, there was no stopping him. Within weeks, he could hold a conversation. When he signed: "Mum" I cried with happiness.

# CHAPTER 48

It was immensely rewarding, watching our little boy grow and progress. And I realised I wanted to help other families, like us.

I took Alex along to the Deafness Resource Centre, in St Helens. I'd been there so many times as a little girl, with Nanny Edith. When I saw it was still running, I felt a rush of nostalgia. I'd had some happy times there.

To my surprise, the woman in charge was a girl I'd played with at the group. We'd been at school together.

"Fancy seeing you here," she grinned.

We got such a warm welcome and immediately, I wanted to get involved. Soon, I was offered the job of family liaison officer, helping other families and their children.

Sadly, I came across teenagers and sometimes adults who were, and always had been, unable to communicate with their parents. As little children, they had been sent far away to specialist boarding schools and then colleges, and so had never really been a part of true family life. Their parents, as a result, had never learned sign-language. The lack of communication caused rifts in families and emotional and mental health problems.

It was heartbreaking. But I relished the opportunity to help.

When Alex was 14 months old, I started a playgroup, supporting deaf children and their families. We'd meet on Tuesday and Thursday mornings, just for a couple of hours, at a local Sure Start centre. We only had five or six families at first. We'd tell stories, teach signing and sing songs. Sometimes we baked biscuits, other times we did arts and crafts. Natalie, Samantha and Cath were a big support. They loved coming along. And all their children learned sign language, too. Everyone helped out.

One of the dads at the group was called Luke. His daughter was profoundly deaf, and I noticed one week that he and Samantha were getting on very well.

"Luke's taking me out this evening," she told me later. "I can't wait. I've fancied him for weeks!"

"I should be running a dating agency, not a playgroup," I joked.

There were other advantages to us all learning sign language, too.

One day, I walked into a café and two young blokes, both deaf, were signing at a corner table. One of them looked over at me, sniggered and signed: "Three out of 10" to his mate.

"The cheek of it!" I fumed, silently.

But I had to resist the urge to laugh, too. What were the chances of them meeting another signer like that?

Whilst Alex and I had a drink and a cake, I watched them giving scores to every woman who walked through the door.

As we left, I tapped one of them on the back of the head and signed: "Actually, my fella thinks I'm Eight out of 10."

Giggling, I pushed Alex's pram out into the street.

"Let that be a lesson to you," I signed to him, though of course he was much too young to understand.

# CHAPTER 49

Gradually, the playgroup merged with a little group at the deafness Resource Centre called 'Happy Hands.' I took over the whole thing, offering help to all families right across the region. It was all run completely by volunteers, so I roped in Cath, Samantha and Natalie to be on my committee.

"I wouldn't dare say no!" Cath grinned.

For me, it was a vocation, not a job. It was immensely challenging and satisfying.

We held regular fun days and charity events, all to raise money for the children.

One day, I climbed Mount Snowdon, as part of a sponsored event for the group, alongside Cath and my daughters.

Another time, we planned a big Happy Hands charity day. Cath and I were up till 3am on the day of the party, baking and icing cakes. That same morning, we were out again by 7am, loading a borrowed van with tables and chairs for our stalls. Cath was dropping with exhaustion, but she manned the Tombola all day long. Natalie was in charge of the water and wine stall and Samantha was a floater. I dressed up as a clown and made half the kids laugh, the other half cry.

All day long, we painted faces, fried burgers and handed out raffle prizes. For me, 'Happy Hands' was like another child. I gave it everything.

Natalie and Samantha loved getting involved, they adored their baby brother and he was spoiled rotten. Alex was like a little firework, a bundle of energy and light. As he grew older, he reminded me more and more of my granddad.

Like my grandad, Alex was stubborn and strong-minded. If he didn't get his own way, he would simply close his eyes, so that he could neither see nor hear any punishment coming his way.

One day, we were visiting my dad, and Alex helped himself to a Mars bar from the fridge.

"Excuse me, that's my Mars Bar," dad signed.

Alex simply closed his eyes, peeled back the wrapper, and ate the whole thing without peeping once.

"It's almost as though your granddad has been reincarnated," my dad smiled. "They are so similar."

It was a huge comfort to us both. I felt like my grandparents were back – and living on through Alex.

# Chapter 50

When Alex was three years old, I began looking around for a suitable nursery and realised, in despair, that there wasn't one. I had seen all too often the devastating results of sending a deaf child into an environment without the right resources. And I wasn't going to let that happen to my son.

I contacted the council and made plans to visit every school in the borough. I even travelled to visit specialist schools in the North East. We spent a whole week at a school in Newcastle-upon-Tyne, which specialised in educating deaf children. I picked up lots of useful information – ammunition for the council. Then, when I finally made my choice, for a school in Knotty Ash, Liverpool, it was rejected.

"I'm not giving up," I vowed. "I mean business."

I was angry, with the council for letting Alex down, and with a world who did not or would not look after its most vulnerable and fragile. I had the tools to fight this. But so many parents didn't. Fired up, I drew up an education care plan for Alex and sent it the local council.

"Like I said," I told them. "I won't give up."

And this time, after arguments back and forth, it was accepted.

"You're off to school like a big boy!" I told Alex.

On his first day, Alex skipped down the school path, his chubby little hand in mine, his face lit up with anticipation, a precious little gemstone, off to share his sparkle with the rest of the world.

It could not have been more different from my own first day at school, and I was very glad. The school receptionist greeted Alex and signed: "Good Morning." It was a good start – and from there, it just got better. Alex loved it. He had one-to-one help, and he seemed to settle in straightaway.

As I waved goodbye, Alex hardly looked up from the sand-pit where he was up to his elbows. He wasn't at all bothered to see me go.

"See ya," he signed, throwing sand everywhere.

I giggled. I had been happy to start school, too – but for a completely different reason to Alex. He had a confidence and a self-assurance that I had worked hard to instil and I could not have been prouder.

Those days were full of sunshine. At weekends, we took the kids out. We had holidays in Tenerife. Strangely for me, it was a settled, contented time. And because life was without drama and chaos, I suddenly started to feel uneasy. Things were going too well, I told myself. There was bound to be trouble around the corner. And so, even on the most uneventful, cooked-breakfast-lazy-day-trip-to the park-Disney-film weekends, there was a constant undercurrent of unease. It was like a verruca. I could live with it. But I knew it was there.

# CHAPTER 51

And then, with the drip-drip-drip of a relationship going sour, Tom and I started to drift apart. It was so subtle at first, it barely registered. In the evenings, with Alex in bed, we might usually have watched a film. Neither of us were big drinkers, but we'd have a brew and biscuits, and chew over the day's events.

But I noticed that Tom seemed disinterested and distant. More often than not, he'd fall asleep mid-conversation.

"Are you sleeping OK?" I asked him. "You're always nodding off."

He shrugged and we left it at that. But I was worried about him, I noticed how quiet he was. I knew he had a lot of stress at work and I wondered whether it was getting to him.

"Maybe you're coming down with something," I said to him. "You never seem to have any energy."

Again, he shrugged. And there was an awkward silence. We didn't seem to have anything to say to each other anymore.

Then, as I was sorting the washing basket one morning, I came across a packet of pills in his pocket. Viagra. My mouth ran suddenly dry. I slapped them onto the kitchen worktop and threw his trousers into the washing machine as though they were diseased.

"Well?" I snapped, when I heard the front door open.

Tom looked momentarily shocked but he covered it with a guilty smile.

"I was going to surprise you," he said. "They're for me and you. This weekend."

I wanted so much to believe him. But I couldn't. Just couldn't. I had a horrible, sickly feeling inside. The last thing I felt like was a night of passion. The weekend came and went and we didn't even sit on the same couch, never mind stay up all night bonking.

And a little voice in my head whispered: "Told you so, Joanne. You cheated on Mark. It's your turn now."

# CHAPTER 52

Our relationship dragged along and sometimes those evenings together, early in 2016, were so lonely. They reminded me of the long nights, when I was little, left home alone whilst mum was out. Nowadays, we had electric and gas. We had money for food. But somehow, it seemed almost as bleak.

It felt like every time I opened my mouth with a bit of news, Tom's eyelids would drop and close, right on cue.

And it slowly dawned on me that he wasn't tired in the evenings at all – he was bored – with me! He would rather fake being asleep than speak to me or watch a film together. I was indignant, outraged even. And then, I felt a terrible, flattening sort of sadness. How had it come to this? We had been through so much, me and him.

"Please don't let me down, Tom," I pleaded silently. "Not you."

Life carried on, day to day, but it was tense. I began secretly checking on him, opening his bank statements, emptying his pockets, searching for what I hoped I would never find. One day in May 2016, he went off to work as usual, and I was getting Alex ready for school. Alex was careering around the house with his usual early-morning enthusiasm, when I noticed Tom had left his email account open.

Unable to stop myself, I began trawling through the list. And when it flashed up, my heart dropped. I had known, all along, it was there. But the shock was cataclysmic, all the same.

As I trawled through his emails, there it was, a message to another woman, confirming he had booked a holiday in Tenerife, for the two of them.

"Tom," I croaked, my whole body shaking. "How could you?"

He and I went every year to Tenerife. We'd even taken Alex, earlier that same year. It had become our regular family holiday. Our place.

It wasn't the same hotel. That was something, I told myself with a grim smile. I knew how lazy Tom was and it would have been just like him to book the same hotel.

Eager for more pain, I googled the hotel. Now that the wound was bleeding, I was keen to rip it further than I could bear.

And when the image flashed up, I gulped in shock. It was the same hotel after all – but had recently changed its name. He was taking his fancy piece to the self-same hotel where he had taken me and Alex a few months earlier.

The gall of the man. I just couldn't believe it.

"And they say romance is dead," I said bitterly.

I couldn't contain myself. I called Tom at work and heard myself screaming.

"It's not true," he babbled. "You've got it all wrong, babe. Honestly."

"I have the email in front of me," I yelled.

"Well," he stuttered. "You shouldn't even be snooping through my emails, it's not legal."

I slammed the phone down. I ran around the house, throwing clothes into bags, my mind running on too many tracks and at too many different speeds.

By the time Tom got home, Alex and I had gone, already installed in Natalie's spare bedroom.

"Save the lecture," I told Natalie, as I dumped my cases in her hallway. "I know, I know."

The truth was, I felt embarrassed. This should have been the other way round, me taking my daughters in after tiffs with their boyfriends. I was too old and too worn out for all this. I thought back to the quiet life I'd enjoyed for those few delicious months. I had known it couldn't last.

Tom texted all through the night and into the next morning, explaining and apologising.

"I just needed some attention," he wrote. "You're so busy all the time."

"Grow up!" I retorted. "For God's sake."

He explained they had met on Tinder.

"And I suppose you were honest and explained you were living with your girlfriend?" I replied.

So that explained the Viagra. The shiftiness. The indifference towards me. God, but I had been such a fool. Once again. Good old Joanne. Nothing if not naïve.

Four weeks passed and we settled into some sort of bumpy routine, of Tom seeing Alex two or three times a week. There was a painful pause when he flew off to Tenerife with his girlfriend. But I told myself, I just had to get used to this. I had been through worse. And I would get through this.

One advantage of my upbringing was that I had learned never to rely completely on anybody. The only person I could really count on was Cath. And so losing Tom was further confirmation of that.

But there was bitterness between us. I could hardly look him in the eye when he came to collect Alex. At first, I didn't even let him into the house. But, as time went on, we began chatting, on the doorstep.

"Just for Alex's sake," I told myself.

But when I heard the door, I found myself checking my hair, in the mirror, before I answered. I looked forward to seeing him. I couldn't help it.

One afternoon, at the end of July, Tom dropped Alex off as usual and was busy telling me all about his antics that day.

"Alex was so funny," he smiled. "Honestly, what a great kid we've got Joa. We really have."

My guard down, I smiled – really smiled – at him. And it was quickly followed by a stab of disappointment. I realised how much I still loved him.

Tom caught the look in my eye and said: "I miss you too, Joa. We've been through a lot together. Too much to throw away."

I swallowed hard.

"Don't do this again, Tom," I pleaded. "You've made your choice."

But it all tumbled out – what an idiot he'd been, how much he missed me and Alex, how he would do anything for a second chance.

"No chance," I told him sharply.

But he could sense I was cracking. I thought of Alex, he was the glue that bound us together. He already had his own personal challenges. Didn't he deserve better than this? I felt like we'd both let him down very badly.

One afternoon in July, Tom dropped Alex off and Alex dragged him into the house, holding tightly onto his arms, and pointed at the chair.

"He wants you to stay," I said.

I made us a coffee and we chatted, with Alex running between us both. It was like old times. And then I heard myself agreeing to a trial run – and there was nobody more surprised than me.

"I won't let you down," Tom said, his eyes bright with happiness. "Let's make this official. Marry me, Joa. Please, I want to prove to you how serious I am."

I laughed in surprise. This was one extreme to another. We had gone from separation to marriage and leap-frogged the whole thing in-between.

The thing was, I had always said I would never get married. I just wasn't the type. I didn't see the need for a piece of paper. Deep down, I was fiercely independent and probably something of a loner, in my own way. I didn't fancy being tied to anyone.

I wasn't one for marshmallow dresses and fancy tiaras either. It was all fluff and nonsense to me.

But I knew how happy Alex would be if we got married. I pictured his little face, beaming.

"A wedding would bring everyone together," Tom wheedled. "Come on, say yes."

I was carried away in the moment and, despite myself, I nodded. Tom swept me up off my feet, and into the air. Alex ran around the living room and waved his hands in excitement. He could sense something was going on.

"Just a small wedding," I said firmly. "You, me and the kids."

But Tom had other ideas.

Before I knew it, he had invited a load of our family and friends. He booked our local cricket club for a reception for 50 guests.

"Let's do this in style," he said.

I hadn't seen him so happy for years. He was rejuvenated, re-energised, like a barmy Groom-zillah. He did all the planning, all the arrangements. Cath's husband, John, offered to drive me to church in his car. I wasn't going to at first, but Tom persuaded me to buy a new dress.

"Treat yourself," he smiled.

I chose a long, strapless, white dress, with long burgundy dresses for the bridesmaids. Despite myself, I started to look forward to the wedding and I got into the spirit of it, ordering a cake and flowers. Cath was good with a camera, and she offered to be our official photographer.

I was touched that Tom was making so much effort. He insisted on paying for everything. But there was one sticking point between us.

"I'm not changing my name," I told him stubbornly.

Tom was a traditional sort, he wanted us both to have the same surname. But I was not prepared to budge.

"I always said I wouldn't change my name for any man and I mean it," I insisted.

Tom sulked. But my mind was made up.

I wanted to keep something of myself separate and intact. And, in the future, I would be so glad I had done so.

# Chapter 53

On the morning of our wedding, August 27, 2016, there was a knock at the door, and I found a driver wearing top hat and tails, waiting outside. Parked in the street was a white vintage wedding car, with champagne chilling inside.

This was obviously Tom's idea of a surprise.

"What's he gone and done now?" I spluttered.

With hindsight, I probably seemed ungrateful. But I was annoyed that he had thrown yet more money at our wedding. And I hated the idea of arriving at the register office in such a fancy car, too.

"Aw, mum, it'll be a laugh," Natalie persuaded me. "Lighten up!"

And she was right. After a glass of champagne, I forgot all about our bank balance. Later that day, Tom and I were married at St Helens register office. Dad walked me down the aisle, Alex was a page boy, my daughters were bridesmaids. Cath and Chris were both there. Mum wasn't invited and neither did she make an appearance. She didn't send a card and that was fine by me. I wasted no time worrying about her at my wedding. Surrounded by everyone I loved, this really felt like a fresh start.

And afterwards, the honeymoon period was, quite literally, a honeymoon period. We were like love-sick teenagers again. We got on so well, laughing and chatting, just like the old days.

Tom seemed interested in me again and, even better, pleased that I was interested in him. It wasn't a lot to ask, but it was everything to me. What more did we need?

We couldn't afford to go away, but instead we were saving to take Alex on holiday with us, early the following year.

Then, in October, both of our cars were stolen during the night. I woke up at 3am to hear Alex shouting, and when I went into his bedroom, he signed: "Mummy, it's cold."

Slowly coming to my senses, I realised he was right,. There was a cold draught whistling up the stairs. I ran down to the hallway, to find our front door was swinging wide open – and the car keys gone.

We were insured of course, and I spent the rest of that week calling the police and organising pay-outs. It wasn't a major problem. But for me, it felt like the tiniest dent in our happiness – the beginning of the slide.

And so, the honeymoon period did not last. The clue, I suppose, was in the name. There were little niggles, and maybe they meant nothing. But with our past history, I found it harder and harder to trust Tom again.

Once or twice a week, I'd babysit for Natalie, when she was working nights. By now, she had a second daughter, Eadie, aged two. It was usually easier if I slept at her house with Alex, rather than bringing her children to me.

But sometimes, when I called Tom to say goodnight, he didn't answer. There were even nights when I couldn't get hold of him at all. I called and texted but there was no reply.

"Where were you?" I asked him the following morning. "I called you five or six times."

"Oh, I was ages at the gym," he replied airily. "It was late when I got home. I thought you'd be asleep."

But I recognised the expression on his face, or I thought I did. I had seen it before – when I found the Viagra tablets in his pocket.

With my heart sinking, I slunk upstairs and searched the dirty washing basket, picking through the sweaty socks and undies. But there was no gym kit. I checked his gym bag and his car boot, loathing myself for it. But it was a compulsion. I slowly began to realise that the affair was not, after all, the worst part. The aftermath was killing me. I hated what I had become, suspicious, devious and neurotic.

The gym kit turned up in the washing machine, Tom thought he'd earn brownie points by washing it himself. I had been wrong to suspect him, after all. But the doubt was like mould, infecting our relationship, spreading silently, ruining everything that was good between us.

One day in late September, I was booked on an interpreting course, and I went outside, already late, to find my tyre was flat.

"Take my car," Tom said, throwing me the keys. "I'll fix this while you're on the course."

Sitting in his car, surrounded by Tom's things, I had an overwhelming urge to snoop. I felt like a little girl again. I closed my eyes and I could see myself, rooting through mum's bedside drawers, and finding the shaving brush. I remembered the tears which had followed. And I knew now, as I opened my eyes, that there were more to come.

What was it about eavesdroppers hearing no good of themselves? Well, I decided grimly, the same could no doubt be said for snooping wives. I emptied the glovebox and did a sweep under the seats. Amongst the wrappers and the rubbish, I found a receipt for a restaurant in Liverpool. I felt my whole body lurch forward, as if I'd set off with the handbrake on.

Feverishly, I checked my diary. I'd been babysitting, overnight, for Natalie on that date.

I called Tom, furious but also strangely resigned.

"Don't you remember, it was my mate's birthday. I told you all about it. It was just a pizza. Where's the harm in that?"

I had a vague recollection. I had to admit. But I knew there would be other times. I knew this would be endless. It was like I was waiting to catch him out. It was just a matter of time. Our relationship teetered on the crest of one slump after another. We had weeks of hardly speaking. And then, there were vicious, screaming rows.

CHAPTER 53

I no longer liked either of us when we were together.

During sleepless nights, I agonised over what had gone wrong. Why was I so rubbish with relationships? I was used to taking shit from my mother. Had I fallen into the same old pattern with men? Was it her fault, or was it mine? Or was it The Middlehurst Curse?

"Damn you, mum," I muttered. "If there is a Middlehurst curse, I hope it gets to you too."

During those bleak months, 'Happy Hands' was my salvation. I needed the group as much as it needed me. When the cold weather came, we planned Halloween parties, trips on the Santa Express and Christmas get-togethers. When the weather warmed up, Cath and I organised days out to Chester Zoo and activity centres. We held a big annual fun day too, to raise funds for the group, with stalls, bouncy castles and face-painting.

I was always in the middle of organising something. And I loved it. By now, I was chairperson and we had over 300 families in the group, reaching out to people right across the UK.

I was so proud of what we'd achieved, but I knew also there was so much more to do.

In the autumn of 2017, I got an email from Children In Need, asking if two of our children would like to go on the programme.

"We're going to be on TV!" I signed to the group.

The kids were all so excited. In September, a BBC crew arrived for a full day of filming. I was on set, translating the children's sign language for the producers. The children, as expected, stole the show. The footage was shown during Children In Need 2017, and both Alex and I stayed up late to watch it on TV.

"There we are mummy," he signed. "On the telly!"

Tears of pride welled in my eyes. So much had gone wrong in my life. I had made bad decisions. Taken dodgy turns. My work with the deaf families was not exactly atonement. I did it because I enjoyed it, and because I wanted to help my son. But it was something very good, coming from something very bad. For the first time in a long time, I was heading in the right direction.

If there was such a thing as redemption, then Happy Hands was mine. But, whilst my work went from strength to strength, my relationship with Tom was on a permanent slide. There were days when I wondered how much lower we could go.

Our evenings were tense, quiet and moody, punctuated only by furious rows. Something, or someone, had to give and go.

# CHAPTER 54

In the summer of 2018, I booked a holiday to Morocco for me, Alex and my dad – without Tom.

"My dad hardly sees Alex," I explained. "It's a chance for them to spend some time together. That's all."

But the truth was, I just didn't want Tom there. I lied to him. Not to spare his feelings, but because it was easier than having another argument with him.

And the holiday, without him, was so peaceful. I hadn't realised what crushing stress I was under until it was lifted. And it was confirmation – if any was needed – that Tom and I were better off apart.

"You need to make a change, Joanne," my dad said shrewdly, as we said our goodbyes at the airport.

It wasn't like him at all to interfere in my personal life. And I realised again how desperate things had got.

Towards the end of 2018, our poor, injured relationship finally fizzled out. There was no big announcement, no final fanfare. Alex and I began sleeping at Natalie's, two, three, then four times a week. Very slowly, bag by bag, I moved my stuff out and into Natalie's spare room. I came home just so that Alex could spend time with his dad. But we were achingly far apart and I knew there was no way back.

"I don't want to be with you," I told him.

My voice was like the tolling of a funeral bell.

Tom hung his head. He knew this was it. He would never have made the decision himself but I suspected he was probably quite relieved.

It was right. But it was hard. I took the last of my things, pulled up outside Natalie's and called Cath, gulping back tears. I had known it was coming but that didn't help at all. The world seemed suddenly very grey and lonely.

"This is for the best, Joa," she told me. "Tom wasn't the right man for you."

She said it with such conviction, as if she'd known for a long time. I remembered back to the moment I'd told her about us getting together – and her warning about me always choosing the wrong men.

I had thought, back then, that she didn't really get it. Now, I realised, it was me who didn't get it. She had known all along that I was going to have my heart broken and it was just a case of when. I realised I should have listened.

# CHAPTER 55

Alex and I are settled in at Natalie's and, for the time being, that's where we'll stay, though I'd like to get my own place soon. I'm working full-time as a family liaison officer for the deaf, as well as running Happy Hands. Alex is busy at school, and our weekends are generally so filled with fun days and sponsored events that we rarely have any spare time.

Through Happy Hands, I have been working with our local MP and also with the Mayor and Mayoress. I'm forever rattling collection buckets and waving sponsor forms at my family and friends.

"Oh not you again," they joke. "You cost us a fortune, Joanne."

Cath recently dressed as Mrs Christmas for our kids' Christmas party, and she was a huge hit. Natalie and Samantha were there too, with their own children.

SILENT SISTERS

I often see Chris and, because he still lives with mum, I always swallow my pride and ask: "How's your mum getting on?"

But if I'm honest, I ask more for his sake than mine. Mum occasionally asks if I will visit her and take Alex, too. She once asked Natalie if I would go and see her. And she also passes messages through Chris.

"Never," I reply. "I will never see her again. It's pointless her asking."

The anger and the bitterness from the trial has subsided now. The wounds have healed. But the scars still remain and they always will.

I don't hate mum. But I certainly don't love her, either. I think she needs specialist medical help.

I will never understand why she hid the births of her children, less still why she carried the bodies around with her. At the very least, it was disrespectful, inhumane and horribly ghoulish. At the very worst, it was one of the darkest crimes imaginable.

We will never know the truth of what happened and why. Those babies are the true skeletons in her closet.

As a parent, she has failed not just Cath, Chris and me, but also the other four babies, our four sisters.

I don't believe she knows the meaning of motherly love.

Cath often wishes, even now, that mum could be different – warm, kind, motherly even. She hankers after an ideal that will never come true. But not me. My experiences have made me who I am today. I don't regret any of it. Through my own harsh childhood, I've learned to cherish my own children. I've learned, through bitter gut-wrenching experience, how precious each little life is.

But that makes what mum did impossible for me to accept.

# EPILOGUE

There's a gaggle of children running around my legs, almost tying my feet in knots as I balance a tray of cupcakes high above their heads.

We're having a fun day for 'Happy Hands' and it's pure, crazy chaos. Just the way I like it.

And as usual, the room is bubbling with the sort of heart-swelling, awe-inspiring energy and courage that makes me feel so grateful to be a part of this.

With my spare hand, I manage to sign: "Jelly and Ice-cream anyone?"

The whole place erupts, children waving their hands, nodding, eyes shining at the promise of a treat.

And it strikes me, certainly not for the first time, how effectively these little ones can communicate. The spoken word is just one tool. Just one. And these kids have got a whole box of alternatives.

For a fleeting moment, I think back to my own childhood and my own family. Hearing wasn't a problem. But did we listen? Never.

We communicated, swapping pleasantries, insults, information; always on the surface, nothing too deep. My conversations with my mum could have been read out like TV listings. We didn't – couldn't – share thoughts, feelings, secrets. They were buried, locked away to fester.

And when it came time to spill the beans, there was blood spilled, too.

Only in court was mum forced to face up to what had happened. And even then, she squirmed and tried to blur the truth.

"Joa! Where's the ice-cream scoop?"

It's Cath, happily ladling out jelly to a dozen eager little faces.

Cath and her kids, Johnny, 17, Connor, 14, and 10-year-old Aaron, are all here to help. Natalie is here with her children, Kiera, 10, Eadie, four, and one-year old Georgia. And Samantha has brought along her little ones too, two-year-old Novah, along with Luke's two children, Lola and Bobby.

I'm such a proud mum and Mum-Pie. As mum's family was nothing to her, mine are everything to me.

Cath and I stick together like glue.

Our lives are as entwined now as they were all those years ago, when I first laid eyes on my new baby sister.

We see each other every day, and Cath babysits Alex, whilst I'm at work. We go on holiday together, two families as one. Course we fall out all the time – but we always fall straight back in.

And what's important, we talk about the lost babies, our silent sisters. We mark their passing. I visit the grave every year, not to mourn or to feel bitter. But I want to remember our sisters. They are a part of us and the way I see it, I can pay tribute to them by living my life openly and proudly – and without secrets.

So that's why 'Happy Hands' is extra-special to me.

Working with deaf children, communication is top of the list. We share everything, each little nuance, verbal or otherwise.

If I can spread the word that it's important to talk – no matter with your mouth, your hands, or your smile, then I'm doing justice to the memory of my four sisters.

I feel as though I'm giving them – and all silent children – a voice with which to be heard.

# ACKNOWLEDGEMENTS

I would like to thank Catherine and Christopher for sharing this journey with me and for all your valuable input over the years.

My children Natalie, Samantha and Alex who make me proud every day. They have and always will be the reason I live and breathe. I love you.

My Dad for always showing me right from wrong and all of his guidance over the years.

My gorgeous grandchildren and nephews for making me smile every day.

Joe and Ann Cusack for all of their very hard work and for putting up with me and believing in me.

Julie for being my rock for so much of my younger life.

All my colleagues at Deafness Resource Centre who I am thankful to call my friends, in particular Helen who stood loyally beside me in the darkest of my hours, I will be forever in your debt.

Des, Harry and John who worked with me at the time of going to press for supporting me through it.

My nan, Edith W Lee and granddad John Lee for being my true inspiration, lifeline and my best friends.

My mother (and her family — may you all be struck with the Middlehurst curse!) for making me the person I am today.


Joe and Ann Cusack have three sons and live in Manchester. They have over 25 years of experience working in newspapers, magazines, and documentaries. Their first ghost-written book, 'Sold In Secret' was published in November 2018.